GROWING THROUGH GRIEF

HOW TO CONTINUE THROUGH CHRIST

PAUL CHAPPELL

All Scripture quotations are taken from the King James Version.
Special emphasis in verses is added.

First published in 2024 by Striving Together Publications, a ministry of Lancaster Baptist Church, Lancaster, CA 93535. Striving Together Publications is committed to providing tried, trusted, and proven books that will further equip local churches to carry out the Great Commission. Your comments and suggestions are valued.

Striving Together Publications
4020 E. Lancaster Blvd.
Lancaster, CA 93535
800.201.7748

Edited by Chris Ralston
Cover Artwork by Dana Thompson

The author and publication team have put forth every effort to give proper credit to quotes and thoughts that are not original with the author. It is not our intent to claim originality with any quote or thought that could not readily be tied to an original source.

ISBN 978-1-59894-535-5 (paperback)

ISBN 978-1-59894-536-2 (ebook)

Printed in the United States of America

CONTENTS

Session 1: Understanding the Journey 1

Session 2: Surrendering to the Process
When I Want to Give Up 21

Session 3: Receiving God's Comfort
When I Am Hurting 45

Session 4: Resting in God's Goodness
When I Question God 69

Session 5: Relying on the Holy Spirit
When I Don't Know What to Do 95

Session 6: Claiming God's Promise
When I Don't Understand 119

Session 7: Trusting God's Faithfulness
When I Feel Afraid 141

Session 8: Embracing God's Grace
When I Feel Weak 163

Session 9: Staying Connected
When I Feel Alone 185

Session 10: Experiencing God's Peace
When I Am Stressed 207

Session 11: Living with Hope
When I am Discouraged 229

Session 12: Following the Good Shepherd
When I Don't Know the Future 253

Prayer Requests 279

Bible Promises for Grieving Christians 283

Endnotes 289

HE IS DESPISED AND REJECTED OF MEN; A MAN OF SORROWS, AND ACQUAINTED WITH GRIEF: AND WE HID AS IT WERE OUR FACES FROM HIM; HE WAS DESPISED, AND WE ESTEEMED HIM NOT. (ISAIAH 53:3)

1 UNDERSTANDING THE JOURNEY

Session Notes

Discussion

Devotional Readings

1. Into the Depths
2. Tears in a Bottle
3. When the Journey Is Too Much
4. Bearing One Another's Burdens
5. In the Cool of the Day

Personal Application

UNDERSTANDING THE JOURNEY

*"Now a certain man was sick, named Lazarus, of Bethany, the town of Mary and her sister
Martha. 2 (It was that Mary which anointed the Lord with ointment, and wiped his feet
with her hair, whose brother Lazarus was sick.) 3 Therefore his sisters sent unto him,
saying, Lord, behold, he whom thou lovest is sick. 4 When Jesus heard that, he said, This
sickness is not unto death, but for the glory of God, that the Son of God might be glorified
thereby. 5 Now Jesus loved Martha, and her sister, and Lazarus. 6 When he had heard
therefore that he was sick, he abode two days still in the same place where he was. 7 Then
after that saith he to his disciples, Let us go into Judaea again." (John 11:1–7)*

INTRODUCTION

____

____

____

*"When Jesus therefore saw her weeping, and the Jews also weeping which came with her,
he groaned in the spirit, and was troubled, 34 And said, Where have ye laid him? They
said unto him, Lord, come and see. 35 Jesus wept." (John 11:33–35)*

*"Grace be to you and peace from God our Father, and from the Lord Jesus Christ. 3 Blessed
be God, even the Father of our Lord Jesus Christ, the Father of mercies, and the God of all
comfort; 4 Who comforteth us in all our tribulation..." (2 Corinthians 1:2–4)*

1. GRIEF IS disruptive

"Therefore his sisters sent unto him, saying, Lord, behold, he whom thou lovest is sick." (John 11:3)

"When he had heard therefore that he was sick, he abode two days still in the same place where he was.... Then said Jesus unto them plainly, Lazarus is dead." (John 11:6, 14)

A Good creation

"And God saw every thing that he had made, and, behold, it was very good. And the evening and the morning were the sixth day." (Genesis 1:31)

"And the LORD God said, It is not good that the man should be alone; I will make him an help meet for him." (Genesis 2:18)

"A friend loveth at all times, and a brother is born for adversity." (Proverbs 17:17)

"Two are better than one; because they have a good reward for their labour. 10 For
if they fall, the one will lift up his fellow: but woe to him that is alone when he
falleth; for he hath not another to help him up." (Ecclesiastes 4:9–10)

Quote: *"There is a God-shaped vacuum in the heart of each man which cannot be satisfied by any created thing, but only by God."*—**Blaise Pascal**

A Bad Fall

"And when the woman saw that the tree was good for food, and that it was pleasant to the eyes, and a tree to be desired to make one wise, she took of the fruit thereof, and did eat, and gave also unto her husband with her; and he did eat." (Genesis 3:6)

"Wherefore, as by one man sin entered into the world, and death by sin; and so death passed upon all men, for that all have sinned:" (Romans 5:12)

"For the wages of sin is death; but the gift of God is eternal life through Jesus Christ our Lord." (Romans 6:23)

A Real Rescue

"But God commendeth his love toward us, in that, while we were yet sinners, Christ died for us." (Romans 5:8)

"For whosoever shall call upon the name of the Lord shall be saved." (Romans 10:13)

"He is despised and rejected of men; a man of sorrows, and acquainted with grief…" (Isaiah 53:3)

"For we have not an high priest which cannot be touched with the feeling of our
infirmities; but was in all points tempted like as we are, yet without sin. 16 Let us
therefore come boldly unto the throne of grace, that we may obtain mercy, and find
grace to help in time of need." (Hebrews 4:15–16)

"So when this corruptible shall have put on incorruption, and this mortal shall
have put on immortality, then shall be brought to pass the saying that is written,
Death is swallowed up in victory. 55 O death, where is thy sting? O grave, where

is thy victory? 56 The sting of death is sin; and the strength of sin is the law. 57 But thanks be to God, which giveth us the victory through our Lord Jesus Christ." (1 Corinthians 15:54–57)

2. GROWTH IS possible

"Then said Martha unto Jesus, Lord, if thou hadst been here, my brother had not died. 22 But I know, that even now, whatsoever thou wilt ask of God, God will give it thee. 23 Jesus saith unto her, Thy brother shall rise again. 24 Martha saith unto him, I know that he shall rise again in the resurrection at the last day. 25 Jesus said unto her, I am the resurrection, and the life: he that believeth in me, though he were dead, yet shall he live: 26 And whosoever liveth and believeth in me shall never die. Believest thou this? 27 She saith unto him, Yea, Lord: I believe that thou art the Christ, the Son of God, which should come into the world." (John 11:21–27)

God Has a Sovereign plan

"Now Jesus loved Martha, and her sister, and Lazarus. 6 When he had heard therefore that he was sick, he abode two days still in the same place where he was" (John 11:5–6)

"Then said Martha unto Jesus, Lord, if thou hadst been here, my brother had not died. . . . 32 Then when Mary was come where Jesus was, and saw him, she fell down at his feet, saying unto him, Lord, if thou hadst been here, my brother had not died." (John 11:21, 32)

"And we know that all things work together for good to them that love God, to them who are the called according to his purpose. 29 For whom he did foreknow, he also did predestinate to be conformed to the image of his Son, that he might be the firstborn among many brethren." (Romans 8:28–29)

God Allows us to grief

"I cried unto God with my voice, even unto God with my voice; and he gave ear unto me. 2 In the day of my trouble I sought the Lord: my sore ran in the night, and ceased not: my soul refused to be comforted. . . . 4 Thou holdest mine eyes waking: I am so troubled that I cannot speak." (Psalm 77:1–2, 4)

"But though he cause grief, yet will he have compassion according to the multitude of his mercies." (Lamentations 3:32)

God Is Faithful to the grieving

"There hath no temptation taken you but such as is common to man: but God is faithful, who will not suffer you to be tempted above that ye are able; but will with the temptation also make a way to escape, that ye may be able to bear it." (1 Corinthians 10:13)

HIS WORD IS POWERFUL

"This is my comfort in my affliction: for thy word hath quickened me." (Psalm 119:50)

HIS PEOPLE ARE HELPFUL

"Bear ye one another's burdens, and so fulfil the law of Christ." (Galatians 6:2)

3. HOPE IS Realistic

"Jesus said unto her, I am the resurrection, and the life: he that believeth in me, though he were dead, yet shall he live:" (John 11:25)

"And when he thus had spoken, he cried with a loud voice, Lazarus, come forth. 44 And he that was dead came forth, bound hand and foot with graveclothes: and his face was bound about with a napkin. Jesus saith unto them, Loose him, and let him go." (John 11:43–44)

We Have hope because of the RESURRECTION

"Blessed be the God and Father of our Lord Jesus Christ, which according to his abundant mercy hath begotten us again unto a lively hope by the resurrection of Jesus Christ from the dead, 4 To an inheritance incorruptible, and undefiled, and that fadeth not away, reserved in heaven for you, 5 Who are kept by the power of God through faith unto salvation ready to be revealed in the last time." (1 Peter 1:3–5)

"If in this life only we have hope in Christ, we are of all men most miserable. 20 But now is Christ risen from the dead, and become the firstfruits of them that slept." (1 Corinthians 15:19–20)

We Have Hope through belief in God's promises

"Jesus said unto her, I am the resurrection, and the life: he that believeth in me,
though he were dead, yet shall he live: 26 And whosoever liveth and believeth
in me shall never die. Believest thou this? 27 She saith unto him, Yea, Lord: I
believe that thou art the Christ, the Son of God, which should come into the world."
(John 11:25–27)

"Jesus therefore again groaning in himself cometh to the grave. It was a cave, and
a stone lay upon it. 39 Jesus said, Take ye away the stone. Martha, the sister of
him that was dead, saith unto him, Lord, by this time he stinketh: for he hath been
dead four days. 40 Jesus saith unto her, Said I not unto thee, that, if thou wouldest
believe, thou shouldest see the glory of God?" (John 11:38–40)

"Now the God of hope fill you with all joy and peace in believing, that ye may abound in hope, through the power of the Holy Ghost." (Romans 15:13)

CONCLUSION

____

____

____

"And God shall wipe away all tears from their eyes; and there shall be no more death, neither sorrow, nor crying, neither shall there be any more pain: for the former things are passed away." (Revelation 21:4)

GROUP DISCUSSION

1. One of the great blessings of life in the body of Christ is having the opportunity to bear one another's burdens. If you feel comfortable doing so, briefly share with one another the loss that has brought each of you to the *Growing through Grief* group.

2. How does God use relationships to minister His grace to us? How can we minister grace to one another as we embark upon "growing through grief" together?

3. What are some ways we can keep the Word of God "coming into our hearts" over the next week?

4. What is one way the group can be praying for you as it relates to grief this week? (A prayer request section is included at the end of this workbook so you can record the requests of other group members.)

SESSION ONE: DAY ONE

INTO THE DEPTHS

I cried unto God with my voice, even unto God with my voice; and he gave ear unto me. In the day of my trouble I sought the Lord: my sore ran in the night, and ceased not: my soul refused to be comforted. I remembered God, and was troubled: I complained, and my spirit was overwhelmed. . . . Thou holdest mine eyes waking: I am so troubled that I cannot speak. (Psalm 77:1-4)

Grief can come upon us suddenly, such as when a friend or loved one is lost in a fatal car crash. Or it can encroach upon us slowly and gradually, as when a spouse slowly slips into dementia. But whether it is sudden or slow, it can become overwhelming. The promise of Psalm 30:5 that "weeping may endure for a night, but joy cometh in the morning" expresses a glorious truth that gives hope in the midst of grief. Still, the daily reality of living with grief can seem like one long, dark "night of the soul."

Sometimes the best we can do in the face of grief is simply to get out of bed and "do the next thing"—an act of defiance against despair and a statement of our confidence in God's goodness and grace regardless of what our emotions are telling us.[1] And that is okay. The suffering caused by grief forces us to lean into our Heavenly Father in ways that we may never have had to do before. As Joni Eareckson Tada observes, "Suffering has a way of heaving you beyond the shallows of life where your faith feels ankle-deep. It casts you out into the fathomless depths of God."[2]

The author of Psalm 77 experienced this "dark night of the soul" acutely. He wondered whether God had cast him off forever and removed His favor (verse 7), whether His mercy and promises had failed (verse 8), and whether God had "forgotten to be gracious" to him (verse 9). In the face of these doubts and fears, the psalmist's only—and best—recourse was to remind himself of what he knew to be true: God had been faithful in the past and would continue to be faithful in the present. "I will remember the years of the right hand of the most High. I will remember the works of the LORD: surely I will remember thy wonders of old. I will meditate also of all thy work, and talk of thy doings."

The key to leaning into our Heavenly Father during times of grief is to intentionally remind ourselves of God's faithfulness to us in the past and to look for signs of His goodness to us in the present. When we do this, we don't necessarily find answers to all our questions—but there, in the "fathomless depths of God," we find His deep love for us, which can sustain us as the waves of grief crash over our heads.

TODAY'S TAKEAWAY

When grief threatens to overwhelm you, lean into the loving arms of your Heavenly Father by recalling His faithfulness to you in the past and His goodness to you in the present.

JOURNAL PROMPT

What are some ways in which God has shown His faithfulness to you in the past? How is He demonstrating His goodness to you in the present?

SESSION ONE: DAY TWO

TEARS IN A BOTTLE

Thou tellest my wanderings: put thou my tears into thy bottle: are they not in thy book? (Psalm 56:8).

Medical experts tell us that when we suffer a wound to our skin—a cut, scrape, surgical incision, or other trauma—our bodies immediately spring into action to begin the process of healing the wound. Typically, the healing process involves four stages.[3] First, the body works to stop any bleeding by forming a blood clot that eventually turns into a scab; this helps to protect the wound and prevent additional blood loss. Second, the body works to heal and clean the wound by allowing extra blood into the area; this blood brings much-needed oxygen, nutrients, and infection-fighting macrophages (white blood cells) to bear on the wound. Inflammation and warmth at the wound site are common during this stage of the healing process. Once the wound has been cleaned and healed, the body can begin rebuilding new skin tissue at the wound site. This is stage three of the healing process. Scarring often occurs at this stage. Finally, in stage four, the body works to rebuild tissue strength at the wound site. All told, depending on the nature of the injury to the skin, the process can take two or more years.

The wound healing process is complex, and healing can be delayed or prevented altogether if certain factors are not present. Two essential factors are oxygen and blood supply. If there are not enough of either of these going to the affected area, the time required for healing can be extended dramatically.

Just as our bodies require time to heal from wounds, so too do our hearts need time to heal from the pain of grief. And we should expect that there will be scarring—that we won't in every way be the same after grief as before. But regardless of the length of our season of grief, we can find hope and comfort in the Word of God that works as a balm to soothe and heal the wounds of our hurting hearts. This is one reason why we need to find ways to keep the Word coming into our hearts during our time of grief.

We can also find comfort and hope in knowing that Jesus Christ—God incarnate, the King of the universe—experienced grief. He wept at Lazarus' gravesite (John 11:35). He was "a man of sorrows, and acquainted with grief." (Isaiah 53:3). God knows and cares about every tear we shed; in fact, as Psalm 56:8 tells us, He collects our tears and puts them in a bottle. Our tears are precious to our Heavenly Father, and He will one day wipe every one of them from our eyes (Revelation 21:4).

In the meantime, though, we grieve. So, what are we to do? Let the healing process take its course. Bathe ourselves in the Word of God, allowing it to strengthen, renew, and restore the hurting parts of our soul. Rest in God's promises and place our confidence in the resurrection of Jesus Christ. And above all, trust His healing presence in our lives even when we cannot see Him at work.

TODAY'S TAKEAWAY

Finding healing from grief can be a long process, but along the way we can rest assured that our Heavenly Father sees every tear we cry, and He cares about each one of them.

JOURNAL PROMPT

As you think back over the past few days (or weeks), have you sensed God's healing or comforting presence in a special way? If so, take a moment to record those special moments so you can remember them as you continue on your journey of grief.

SESSION ONE: DAY THREE

WHEN THE JOURNEY IS TOO MUCH

And the angel of the LORD came again the second time, and touched him, and said, Arise and eat; because the journey is too great for thee. (1 Kings 19:7)

The sun beat down on the woman and her child as they trudged through the hot desert sands. Out of water and near the point of exhaustion, the woman laid her son on the ground and sat down a bowshot's distance away, fully expecting him to die of thirst and starvation in the merciless wilderness. As she listened to her son crying, the woman began to sob herself. But then, she heard a voice from heaven: "What aileth thee, Hagar? fear not; for God hath heard the voice of the lad where he is. Arise, lift up the lad, and hold him in thine hand; for I will make him a great nation" (Genesis 21:17–18). Suddenly, God "opened her eyes" and she saw a well, from which she was able to draw water to nourish her son (Genesis 21:19). When the journey was too much for Hagar and Ishmael, God heard . . . and provided the sustenance they needed in that moment.

Elijah the prophet was terrified. Queen Jezebel had threatened to kill him (1 Kings 19:2)—and Jezebel didn't make empty threats. So Elijah ran. He ran a full day's journey into the wilderness where he finally collapsed under a juniper tree (1 Kings 19:4). Despairing, he asked God to take his life and then, in his exhaustion, fell asleep. Later, an angel of the Lord woke him up. "Arise and eat," the angel said, pointing to the food and water that now (miraculously) appeared near Elijah's head. After eating and drinking, Elijah went back to sleep. The angel woke him up a second time, saying, "Arise and eat; because the journey is too great for thee" (1 Kings 19:7). This time, Elijah's strength was renewed—so much so that he was able to travel another forty days and forty nights to reach Mount Horeb. When the journey was too much for Elijah, God saw . . . and provided the strength that Elijah needed to go on.

When Elijah arrived at Mount Horeb, he took refuge in a cave. "What doest thou here, Elijah?" the Lord asked him (1 Kings 19:9). Elijah explained his predicament: "I, even I only, am left; and they seek my life, to take it away" (1 Kings 19:10). Elijah felt utterly alone and completely vulnerable. In response, the Lord revealed Himself to Elijah—but not in the dramatic way one might expect. He didn't reveal Himself in the mighty wind, or the earthquake, or the fire (v. 11). Instead, He revealed Himself in a gentle, "still small voice" (v. 12). When the journey was too much for Elijah, God spoke . . . and gave Elijah what he needed most: His presence.

The journey of grief can be crushing. Some days, you may not feel like going on: What's the point?" you may wonder. When the journey of grief becomes too much for you, know that the Lord of heaven hears the cry of your heart. He sees the hardness of the way. And He speaks to you through His Word. He will provide you with the sustenance you need, the strength to go on, and His personal presence to sustain you. "Wait upon the Lord," as Isaiah 40:31 puts it, and your strength will be renewed.

God's voice may speak to you in a whisper—but speak to you He will. Listen for His voice.

TODAY'S TAKEAWAY

Listen for God's "still small voice" in the midst of your grief; as you do, He will sustain, refresh, and renew you for the journey ahead.

JOURNAL PROMPT

What Bible verse or passage has God been using to speak to you in this season? (Perhaps it is even one from this week's *Growing through Grief* session.) What are the things you need to say to the Lord (even those things you think you "shouldn't" say, feel, or believe)? Pour out your heart to Him honestly. He cares.

SESSION ONE: DAY FOUR

BEARING ONE ANOTHER'S BURDENS

Bear ye one another's burdens, and so fulfil the law of Christ. (Galatians 6:2)

In J. R. R. Tolkien's beloved *Lord of the Rings* saga, there is a famous scene in which Samwise Gamgee makes a pledge to his best friend and dearest companion, Frodo Baggins, that he will stay at Frodo's side no matter what challenges or obstacles await them on their journey. "I made a promise, Mr. Frodo," Samwise says. "A promise. 'Don't you leave him, Samwise Gamgee.' And I don't mean to." Though Frodo struggles under the weight of a great burden, he finds comfort and strength in the words of his faithful friend; his burden is lightened just enough to continue on.

In order to succeed, athletic teams must work together toward a common goal. Each team member plays a vital role in achieving that goal, and winning will prove elusive if some teammates have a higher level of commitment than others. Sometimes, though, a player is injured, in which case the other team members must work even harder to accomplish the goal. But when the team wins, all of its members win—including the one who was injured. They are a team, and together they rise or fall. So, when one teammate is unable to do what needs to be done, the rest "pitch in" to get the job done.

In mountain climbing, a "belay system" is used, in which a climber is connected by a system of ropes and other equipment to someone else (the "belayer") below him. Should the climber lose his footing and fall, the tension in the ropes connecting them enables the belayer to arrest the climber's fall and assist him in regaining his footing.

Loyal friendship. Practical assistance. Help regaining our footing after we've fallen down. These are things we all need in our lives—especially during times of grief. And for followers of Jesus, they are meant to be found especially in the church, Christ's body.

The hard thing is that in the midst of our grief, our natural tendency is often to retreat, to withdraw within ourselves, to "go it alone" in the midst of our pain. This is a normal response, but in doing so we cut ourselves off from one of the most important resources we need as we journey through grief: our brothers and sisters in Christ.

In our time of grief, we need to remember that "there is a friend that sticketh closer than a brother" (Proverbs 18:24), and "a threefold cord is not quickly broken" (Ecclesiastes 4:12). God designed the church to be the sort of place where we can be supported in our weakest times by the strong cords of faithful friendship and Spirit-enabled kinship that comes from being fellow members of His family, the body of Christ.

"Bear ye one another's burdens, and so fulfil the law of Christ," the Apostle Paul said to the believers in Galatia (Galatians 6:2). Sometimes, the hardest thing for us to do is to allow others to share the weight of our burdens. But do so we must. For just as Christ bore our burden of sin on His cross, so we must bear one another's burdens as we take up our crosses and follow Him (Matthew 16:24–26).

TODAY'S TAKEAWAY

As you walk through the valley of grief, resist the temptation to "go it alone." Instead, allow your fellow brothers and sisters the privilege of bearing your burdens with you and thus fulfilling the command to "love one another" as He has loved us (John 13:34–35).

JOURNAL PROMPT

Are you struggling with allowing fellow believers to help you bear the weight of grief? If so, ask the Lord to show you some practical ways in which you might be able to allow them the opportunity to shoulder your burdens along with you.

____

____

____

____

____

____

SESSION ONE: DAY FIVE

IN THE COOL OF THE DAY

And they heard the voice of the Lord God walking in the garden in the cool of the day. (Genesis 3:8)

When God created Adam and Eve, He placed them in an optimal environment—the Garden of Eden—in which all their needs were met. It was a lush garden, watered by a river and populated by trees that were "pleasant to the sight, and good for food" (Genesis 2:9). But then, the worst possible thing happened: the Fall (Genesis 3). Adam and Eve, our human ancestors, rebelled against God and brought themselves and the world under the curse of sin.

In the wake of their disobedience, "the eyes of them both were opened, and they knew that they were naked; and they sewed fig leaves together, and made themselves aprons" (Genesis 3:7). Fear engulfed them, and they "hid themselves from the presence of the Lord God amongst the trees of the garden" (Genesis 3:8). The very trees that had once offered refreshment and sustenance now became a place of hiding from their shame and guilt and even from their Creator. How would He respond?

Perhaps surprisingly, it was God who took the initiative to reach out to Adam and Eve in the midst of their fear, grief, and sorrow. Walking "in the garden in the cool of the day . . . the Lord God called unto Adam, and said unto him, Where art thou?" (Genesis 3:9). It's worth pausing to note this fact: after the tragedy of the Fall, after the worst possible thing had happened . . . God met Adam and Eve where they were at. In the moments that followed, He graciously provided for their immediate needs (verse 21) and offered hope for the future (verses 14–15).

In the book of Revelation, the New Jerusalem, a garden city, is pictured descending from heaven to the new earth (Revelation 21:2). Once again, human beings will dwell in close fellowship with their creator: "He will dwell with them, and they shall be his people . . ." (Revelation 21:3). Like the Garden of Eden, this city will have a river flowing through it, and it will be populated with trees that have leaves for healing (Revelation 22:1–2). People will live at peace with God and in harmony with each other. All our needs will be met; "God shall wipe away all tears from their eyes; and there shall be no more death, neither sorrow, nor crying, neither shall there be any more pain: for the former things are passed away" (Revelation 21:4).

Humanity began in a garden, and eternity will begin with blessed life in a garden city. For now, though, we live in-between those two realities, where there is pain, and sorrow, and death, and grief. As we live with the reality of life between Eden and eternity, we can find comfort in knowing that even though the "worst possible thing" may have happened to us—the death of a child, the collapse of a marriage, the failure of a business venture—we can rest assured that God will meet us where we are. He will walk with us "in the cool of the day," meeting our needs and providing hope for the future.

TODAY'S TAKEAWAY

Even in the midst of our grief, we can experience moments of fellowshipping with God "in the garden in the cool of the day"—and those moments can give us hope for the future.

JOURNAL PROMPT

The journey of grief can sometimes feel loud and chaotic; at other times it can feel sad and lonely. Take a few moments to quiet your soul before the Lord. Invite Him to meet you where you are as you walk together "in the cool of the day." Ask Him to meet your immediate needs and give you hope for the future. What words of comfort do you hear Him speaking to you now?

PERSONAL APPLICATION

The following exercises are intended to give you practical and personal ways to apply the truths you're learning and discussing in the group meetings and daily devotionals. They don't have to be done in any particular sequence or on a particular day of the week. If you only have the physical or emotional energy to complete one of these exercises, that's fine. The point is to allow the Spirit of God to minister to your heart during this time of grief.

INVITING PEOPLE INTO YOUR JOURNEY

As difficult as it can be sometimes, staying connected with other people is a crucial component of responding to grief in a healthy way.

Different people play different roles in the way they help us carry the burden of grief. But we also have a role in being responsive and transparent as people reach out to us.

Take a few moments to consider this question: who are the most significant relationships in your life?

____

____

____

Are there people on this list who are not safe or trustworthy, demonstrate poor boundaries, or place unrealistic expectations on you? Have you given yourself permission to not let them into the journey of grief with you?

Who are the people on this list that, when you are with them, you can take a deep breath and your heart feels at rest? What can you do to build stronger connections with them?

____

____

____

- ○ **Action Item:** Contact one person this week (other than your spouse) and ask them to be part of your journey of grief. Give him/her permission to check on you regularly—and promise them that you will always answer honestly when they ask how you are doing.

STEPPING BACK

Depending on your circumstances, the reason for your grief may have created legal issues, relational demands, or other responsibilities that consume time, resources, and physical or emotional energy.

Are there activities that for a season need to be put on pause to create space for healthy connection and added responsibilities?

- ○ **Action Item:** Write down one area of life that may need a pause for now. What needs to happen in order for that pause to happen? Choose one step that you can accomplish this week to move toward implementing the pause.

____

____

____

STABILIZING YOUR SOUL

Even in the midst of grief, faith and joy can be chosen. When your world feels like it is reeling out of control, it is important to intentionally take steps to stabilize your soul.

- ○ **Action Item:** Go somewhere you really enjoy (the bathtub, a coffee shop, a baseball field, the garden, a park, the beach, etc.). Take with you one tangible item that brings simple comfort, such as a blanket or a cup of coffee (or both). Allow yourself at least thirty minutes of quiet time to reflect on the truths and Scriptures that are sustaining you right now. And, if you find yourself falling asleep . . . just let the Lord give you rest.

BUT LET PATIENCE HAVE HER PERFECT WORK, THAT YE MAY BE PERFECT AND ENTIRE, WANTING NOTHING. (JAMES 1:4)

2

SURRENDERING TO THE PROCESS

WHEN I WANT TO GIVE UP

Session Notes

Discussion

Devotional Readings

1. Experiencing Joy in Times of Sadness
2. When Faith Is Tried
3. Out of the Whirlwind
4. Running the Race
5. Conformed to His Image

Personal Application

SURRENDERING TO THE PROCESS

*"James, a servant of God and of the Lord Jesus Christ, to the twelve tribes which are
scattered abroad, greeting. 2 My brethren, count it all joy when ye fall into divers
temptations; 3 Knowing this, that the trying of your faith worketh patience. 4 But let
patience have her perfect work, that ye may be perfect and entire, wanting nothing.
5 If any of you lack wisdom, let him ask of God, that giveth to all men liberally, and
upbraideth not; and it shall be given him. 6 But let him ask in faith, nothing wavering.
For he that wavereth is like a wave of the sea driven with the wind and tossed. 7 For let
not that man think that he shall receive any thing of the Lord. 8 A double minded man
is unstable in all his ways."* (James 1:1–8)

INTRODUCTION

____

____

____

"For whom he did foreknow, he also did predestinate to be conformed to the image of his Son, that he might be the firstborn among many brethren." (Romans 8:29)

"Mine eyes do fail with tears, my bowels are troubled, my liver is poured upon the earth, for the destruction of the daughter of my people; because the children and the sucklings swoon in the streets of the city." (Lamentations 2:11)

*"For my days are consumed like smoke, and my bones are burned as an hearth. 4 My heart
is smitten, and withered like grass; so that I forget to eat my bread. 5 By reason of the voice
of my groaning my bones cleave to my skin. 6 I am like a pelican of the wilderness: I am like
an owl of the desert. . . . 11 My days are like a shadow that declineth; and I am withered
like grass."* (Psalm 102:3–6, 11)

"James, a servant of God and of the Lord Jesus Christ, to the twelve tribes which are scattered abroad, greeting." (James 1:1)

1. A HEAVENLY ____________________

*"My brethren, count it all joy when ye fall into divers temptations; 3 Knowing this,
that the trying of your faith worketh patience."* (James 1:2–3)

"Being confident of this very thing, that he which hath begun a good work in you will perform it until the day of Jesus Christ:" (Philippians 1:6)

"Knowing this, that the trying of your faith worketh patience." (James 1:3)

The Development of Faith

Quote: *"Untested faith is unreliable faith."*

The Development of Endurance

"Knowing this, that the trying of your faith worketh patience." (James 1:3)

"And not only so, but we glory in tribulations also: knowing that tribulation worketh patience;" (Romans 5:3)

"But as for you, ye thought evil against me; but God meant it unto good, to bring to pass, as it is this day, to save much people alive." (Genesis 50:20)

2. A BIBLICAL Process

Surrender to the Father

"But let patience have her perfect work, that ye may be perfect and entire, wanting nothing." (James 1:4)

"Saying, Father, if thou be willing, remove this cup from me: nevertheless not my will, but thine, be done." (Luke 22:42)

"And being in an agony he prayed more earnestly: and his sweat was as it were great drops of blood falling down to the ground." (Luke 22:44)

"Humble yourselves therefore under the mighty hand of God, that he may exalt you in due time: 7 Casting all your care upon him; for he careth for you." (1 Peter 5:6–7)

"Seeing then that we have a great high priest, that is passed into the heavens, Jesus the Son of God, let us hold fast our profession. 15 For we have not an high priest which cannot be touched with the feeling of our infirmities; but was in all points tempted like as we are, yet without sin. 16 Let us therefore come boldly unto the throne of grace, that we may obtain mercy, and find grace to help in time of need." (Hebrews 4:14–16)

"Wherefore he is able also to save them to the uttermost that come unto God by him, seeing he ever liveth to make intercession for them." (Hebrews 7:25)

Quote: *"If I could hear Christ praying for me in the next room, I would not fear a million enemies. Yet distance makes no difference. He is praying for me."* **—Robert Murray M'Cheyne**

"And lest I should be exalted above measure through the abundance of the revelations, there was given to me a thorn in the flesh, the messenger of Satan to buffet me, lest I should be exalted above measure. 8 For this thing I besought the Lord thrice, that it might depart from me. 9 And he said unto me, My grace is sufficient for thee: for my strength is made perfect in weakness. Most gladly therefore will I rather glory in my infirmities, that the power of Christ may rest upon me. 10 Therefore I take pleasure in infirmities, in reproaches, in necessities, in persecutions, in distresses for Christ's sake: for when I am weak, then am I strong." (2 Corinthians 12:7–10)

Request God's wisdom

"If any of you lack wisdom, let him ask of God, that giveth to all men liberally, and upbraideth not; and it shall be given him." (James 1:5)

Quote: *"The doorstep to the temple of wisdom is a knowledge of our own ignorance."***—Charles Spurgeon**

THREE WAYS GOD GIVES DIVINE WISDOM

1. ***His Word***

   "The law of the LORD is perfect, converting the soul: the testimony of the Lord is sure, making wise the simple." (Psalm 19:7)

2. ***His People***

   "He that walketh with wise men shall be wise: but a companion of fools shall be destroyed." (Proverbs 13:20)

3. ***His Spirit***

   "Howbeit when he, the Spirit of truth, is come, he will guide you into all truth: for he shall not speak of himself; but whatsoever he shall hear, that shall he speak: and he will shew you things to come." (John 16:13)

"But let him ask in faith, nothing wavering. For he that wavereth is like a wave of the sea driven with the wind and tossed." (James 1:6)

Quote: *"Trials are medicines which our gracious and wise Physician prescribes because we need them; and he proportions the frequency and weight of them to what the case requires. Let us trust his skill and thank him for his prescription."* **—Isaac Newton**

"Trust in the LORD with all thine heart; And lean not unto thine own understanding. 6 In all thy ways acknowledge him, And he shall direct thy paths." (Proverbs 3:5–6)

3. A DESIRED Product

"But let patience have her perfect work, that ye may be perfect and entire, wanting nothing." (James 1:4)

"But the God of all grace, who hath called us unto his eternal glory by Christ Jesus, after that ye have suffered a while, make you perfect, stablish, strengthen, settle you." (1 Peter 5:10)

"A double minded man is unstable in all his ways." (James 1:8)

"And the very God of peace sanctify you wholly; and I pray God your whole spirit and soul and body be preserved blameless unto the coming of our Lord Jesus Christ." (1 Thessalonians 5:23)

CONCLUSION

"And we know that all things work together for good to them that love God, to them who are the called according to his purpose. 29 For whom he did foreknow, he also did predestinate to be conformed to the image of his Son, that he might be the firstborn among many brethren." (Romans 8:28–29)

"But we all, with open face beholding as in a glass the glory of the Lord, are changed into the same image from glory to glory, even as by the Spirit of the Lord." (2 Corinthians 3:18)

DISCUSSION

1. Was there anything from last week's devotionals or application exercises that was particularly meaningful or helpful to you? What passage of Scripture has been most reassuring to you this past week?

2. As you look back over your life up to this point, can you identify periods of personal or spiritual growth? What were some of the key factors that helped to bring about change?

3. What are some of the characteristics of Christlikeness in a Christian? How have you seen God use trials to develop these characteristics in yours or other people's lives?

4. What is one way the group can pray for you as it relates to grief this week?

SESSION TWO: DAY ONE

EXPERIENCING JOY IN TIMES OF SADNESS

Rejoice evermore. Pray without ceasing. In every thing give thanks: for this is the will of God in Christ Jesus concerning you. (1 Thessalonians 5:16-18)

We are told in 1 Thessalonians 5:16 to "rejoice evermore"—to continually choose to rejoice. But how is this possible, especially when we feel overwhelmed by grief? The key to this is understanding that joy and happiness are not the same thing.

Happiness and joy do share similarities with one another. Both are emotional states that typically involve feelings of pleasure, delight, satisfaction, and contentment. Indeed, our dictionaries often define the concepts interdependently and in nearly synonymous ways.

Still, despite their close relationship, happiness and joy are not identical. Happiness is related to our circumstances, and circumstances inevitably change. It comes and goes on the tides of life's experiences.

Joy—true, biblical joy—on the other hand, runs deeper. It is not rooted in our circumstances but in who God is and who we are in relation to Him. It is focused on God's promises and His faithfulness.

Joy-filled Christians acknowledge the reality of painful circumstances, but they also recognize God's sovereignty and affirm His goodness—even in the face of apparent evidence to the contrary. As one person put it, "Happiness is a reaction to something great. Joy is the product of someone great."[1] Jesus is that Someone to whom we turn in the midst of our sadness and grief—and in whom we can find joy we never imagined possible.

Jesus experienced profound grief, sorrow, and sadness during his sojourn here on earth. He wept at Lazarus' death (John 11:35), lamented the stubbornness of fallen human hearts who refused to come to Him

(Matthew 23:37), and, as He hung on the cross, experienced the anguish of taking the sins of the world upon Himself: "My God, my God, why hast thou forsaken me?" (Matthew 27:46).

Yet, Jesus also experienced joy—indeed, it was "the joy that was set before him" (Hebrews 12:2) that motivated Him to endure the cross and the shame it brought on our behalf. The moments of suffering that Jesus experienced—culminating in the agony of the cross—were surely not "happy times" for Him. There was nothing about Jesus' experience on the cross that could be considered pleasant or fun. Still, the knowledge that His life, death, and resurrection would make it possible for humankind's relationship with God to be restored provided Jesus with a deep, abiding joy that enabled Him to endure even in the face of profound grief. Jesus' life provides us with a model of how to persevere—with joy—in the midst of our own seasons of grief, sorrow, and pain.

The good news is that in the midst of our grief, we don't have to try to fake being happy. God never asks us to do this. Instead, we are instructed to rejoice. This is not a feeling, but a choice.

How do we do this? The next two verses in the passage give us a clue. We pray—without ceasing. And we intentionally give thanks to God—even when we don't feel like doing so. Prayer and thankfulness turn our attention toward God and His goodness to us. As we acknowledge His presence and provision in our lives, we are empowered to rejoice even as we grieve.

TODAY'S TAKEAWAY

Through prayer and thankfulness, we can experience joy even in times of sadness.

JOURNAL PROMPT

To pray without ceasing and to give thanks in everything requires intention. What items or activities that are part of your normal day can serve as a reminder to you to pray? What is one way you can add the purposeful giving of thanks into your daily routines?

SESSION TWO: DAY TWO

WHEN FAITH IS TRIED

Knowing this, that the trying of your faith worketh patience. But let patience have her perfect work, that ye may be perfect and entire, wanting nothing. (James 1:3–4)

When our faith is tried, God develops the fruit of endurance in our lives. By His grace, He gives us the willingness and ability to continue with steadfastness in the face of hardship. And God uses this process to develop spiritual maturity in us.

While God is always interested in growing us into maturity, the practical reality is that our seasons of trial can be particularly effective at growing us. We may wonder why God couldn't use a less painful way of growing us into spiritual maturity. C. S. Lewis wondered that. In his profound grief over the death of his wife, Lewis at one point likened God to an "Eternal Vet" who seemed to have a penchant for inflicting "operations even more painful than our severest imaginings can forebode." Yet, with time, Lewis found himself simultaneously with the growing conviction that, in the end, "all shall be well, and all shall be well, and all manner of thing shall be well."[2]

How did he arrive at this conviction? In part, it was the result of a realization that many of his prior ideas about God's goodness had been grossly insufficient. God's goodness was, it turned out, consistent with allowing pain—even severe pain—into his life. But even in the midst of the unanswerable "why?" questions, Lewis discovered God could be trusted, and that is why he could conclude that, ultimately, "all shall be well." Lewis had learned the truth that untested faith is unreliable faith. As he put the point,

> You never know how much you really believe anything until its truth or falsehood becomes a matter of life and death to you. It is easy to say you believe a rope to be strong and sound as long as you are merely using it to cord a box. But suppose you had to hang by that rope over a precipice. Wouldn't you then first discover how much you really trusted it?[3]

In the end, "only a real risk tests the reality of a belief."[4]

Grief, perhaps like nothing else, forces us to make a choice: will we lean into our faith in God, or will we turn away from Him in bitterness and resentment? Will we trust in God's promises even when we can't see to the bottom of the chasm of grief that threatens to swallow us from below?

The good news is this: God's promises spring from His good nature, which is eternally unchanging—and, therefore, utterly secure and reliable. Stepping forward in faith may not always *appear* to be the safest path, but as it turns out, that is the one sure way to make it to the other side of the chasm of grief with hope intact.

TODAY'S TAKEAWAY

Stepping forward in faith is the surest way to maintain hope in the face of grief.

JOURNAL PROMPT

Are you struggling to trust in God's goodness during this time of grief? The best path forward is to talk with God honestly about those areas and to ask Him to reveal to you His good and loving character in a fresh way. One exercise to help is to complete the following sentences—as many times as needed.

Dear God, I am struggling to see your goodness in/when . . .

But this is what I know to be true about your love and character:

Dear God, I am struggling to see your goodness in/when . . .

But this is what I know to be true about your love and character:

SESSION TWO: DAY THREE

OUT OF THE WHIRLWIND

And [Job] said, Naked came I out of my mother's womb, and naked shall I return thither: the LORD gave, and the LORD hath taken away; blessed be the name of the LORD. (Job 1:21)

Job had lost nearly everything—his children, his livestock, his wealth, possessions, and reputation. In response, he grieved; he "rent his mantle, and shaved his head" (Job 1:20). But then he did something peculiar: he "fell down upon the ground, and worshipped" (Job 1:20). "Naked came I out of my mother's womb," he said, "and naked shall I return thither: the LORD gave, and the LORD hath taken away; blessed be the name of the LORD" (Job 1:21).

Shortly thereafter, Satan was permitted to afflict Job with boils that covered his entire body, causing agonizing and unrelenting pain. Job's wife encouraged Job to "curse God, and die" (Job 2:9). In response, Job asked, "What? shall we receive good at the hand of God, and shall we not receive evil?" (Job 2:10).

Later, as Job mourned the loss of his family and continued to experience excruciating physical pain, three of his friends—Eliphaz, Bildad, and Zophar—attempted to provide explanations for why Job was suffering. Surely, they argued, Job must have done something to deserve this suffering; surely, he *must* have sinned. After all, according to their view of how God operates, the righteous are always rewarded and the wicked are always punished. Thus, if someone is rewarded, God must see them as righteous, and if someone is suffering, God must be punishing them. In response, Job vehemently insisted on his innocence and told them that their explanations of his predicament simply didn't add up. Not only that, Job also launched a series of complaints against God. What God had permitted didn't make sense to Job, and it certainly didn't seem fair.

Interestingly enough, when God finally did respond to Job's complaints, He didn't directly answer any of the "why?" questions raised by Job or his companions. Instead, "the LORD answered Job out of the whirlwind, and said, Who is this that darkeneth counsel by words without knowledge?" (Job 38:1–2). He then confronted Job with example after example of His divine, creative power and sovereign control over the entire creation and all that happens in it. In response to Job's questions, God did not offer the individual answers Job was seeking; instead, He offered Himself. And in the end, that was enough for Job: "I uttered that I understood not; things too wonderful for me, which I knew not" (Job 42:3).

When we've lost everything, the most counterintuitive thing to do is to praise the Lord. But that's exactly what Job did (in Job 1:31). And it's what we must do, too. Grief, pain, worship, and praise can and must coexist. Worship and praise can also coexist with our unanswered questions. For it is there—in the midst of the "whirlwind" of life this side of eternity—that God meets us, reminding us of who He is in all His awesome power and loving sovereignty. And that is enough.

TODAY'S TAKEAWAY

In the face of our grief, pain, and unanswered questions, we can rely on the truth that God remains sovereign—and we can respond with praise, knowing that His presence is *the* answer we ultimately seek.

JOURNAL PROMPT

What is one thing for which you can praise the Lord today? (Questions to help get you started include these: Has anything happened to you recently that reminded you of God's sovereignty or His presence with you? What is an attribute of His nature that you know is unchanging? What is a Scripture passage that God has provided to give you hope?) You'll want to record your answers to these questions so you can remember them later when you are in the whirlwind of grief.

SESSION TWO: DAY FOUR

RUNNING THE RACE

Wherefore seeing we also are compassed about with so great a cloud of witnesses, let us lay aside every weight, and the sin which doth so easily beset us, and let us run with patience the race that is set before us, (Hebrews 12:1)

James 1:3 tells us that "the trying of [our] faith worketh patience," and Romans 5:3 informs us that "tribulation worketh patience." As anyone who's gone on a long road trip or airplane flight with young children knows well, patience doesn't come easy to us. *Are we there yet? When can we stop? I'm hungry; when are we going to eat?* The questions go on and on.

The patience that God develops in our lives through suffering is about more than simply putting up with the kids fighting in the back seat of the car or the annoying coworker who never seems to stop talking. It deals with endurance—the ability to hold up under pressure over the long term.

Whether we're on a road trip or running a marathon, we won't reach our destination instantly. Destinations worth pursuing take time and, often, great effort to reach. The same is true of personal goals. There is time between our intention and our accomplishment.

The swimmer Florence Chadwick, who we met in this week's lesson, didn't succeed at swimming the English or Catalina Channels quickly or easily. Both achievements were the result of extensive training, resolute endurance, and—in the case of the Catalina Channel—her willingness to try again after failing.

A similar dynamic exists in our spiritual growth. It takes time to develop spiritual maturity. This is why the author of the book of Hebrews exhorts us to "run with patience the race that is set before us, looking unto Jesus the author and finisher of our faith" (Hebrews 12:1–2).

But what does it mean to "run with patience the race that is set before us" when we're in the midst of a season of grief? Surely, it doesn't mean having to pretend that we "have it all together" or that we understand what's happening to us, or even that we know where we're headed. It simply means asking God what next step of faithfulness, trust, and obedience He would have us take. And when we're struggling with grief, we may only be able to answer that question one day at a time.

We can take this "next step" by asking the Lord, "what do you want me to do *today*?" In our time of grief, the answer may very well be, "Rest. Rest in My presence. Rest in My arms for a while." That, too, is part of running "the race that is set before us" with patient endurance.

TODAY'S TAKEAWAY

The Christian life is a long journey of faithfulness, trust, and obedience. Even in the midst of a season of grief, we can take the next step on that journey by asking the Lord, "what do You want me to do *today*?

JOURNAL PROMPT

Do you sense the Lord prompting you toward a particular step of faithfulness, trust, or obedience? As you come to the Lord in prayer, ask Him to show you how to take that step even as you continue to grieve. Record here what you sense the Lord is asking you to do, and what He is showing you about how to take that step. Then, rest in His promise that He is with you and will enable you to do what He is asking of you.

SESSION TWO: DAY FIVE

CONFORMED TO HIS IMAGE

For whom he did foreknow, he also did predestinate to be conformed to the image of his Son, that he might be the firstborn among many brethren. (Romans 8:29)

We are, as Genesis 1:26–27 tells us, made "in God's image." But what does this mean, and how does it relate to our experience of grief?

One way to think about the image of God in every human is in terms of a blueprint. In the same way that a building resembles the architect's design, so we have a special connection with and reflect or resemble the one who designed us, namely God Himself. The image of God in us is limited and confined to certain aspects of our makeup. But Scripture tells us that Jesus is the "express image" of God (Hebrews 1:3) and "the image of the invisible God" (Colossians 1:15). If we want to know what God is like, we should look first and foremost to Jesus.

Importantly, as we consider what Jesus—God in the flesh—is like, we are confronted immediately with the fact that He suffered. Indeed, He was the Suffering Servant, described in Isaiah 53 as "a man of sorrows, and acquainted with grief" (Isaiah 53:3).

Hebrews 5:8 tells us about Jesus, "Though he were a Son, yet learned he obedience by the things which he suffered." If Jesus grew in the human aspects of spiritual maturity through suffering, we can expect that God will bring maturity into our lives through suffering as well. As we, like Jesus, surrender to the will of the Father and hope with patient endurance for His work in our lives, He will conform us to the image of Christ.

For those of us who are experiencing the pain and sorrow of grief, this is truly good news. It reminds us that God is not only *for* us in our suffering, but that He is *with* us. He truly understands what we are experiencing.

And because we, His children, are—through the process of sanctification—being "conformed to the image of his Son" (Romans 8:29), we, too, will share in the life that He secured through His death and resurrection.

Because Christ lives, we have hope—*true* hope.

TODAY'S TAKEAWAY

Because God became one of us and suffered like us, we can rest assured that He is unequivocally *with* us and *for* us in the midst of our suffering.

JOURNAL PROMPT

What are some specific ways in which God has shown Himself to be *with* you and *for* you in this time of grief? Take a few moments to record these gracious gifts from God. As you go to Him in prayer, thank Him in writing for being present with you in your suffering and ask Him to remind you of the hope that Jesus' resurrection provides.

PERSONAL APPLICATION

The following exercises are intended to give you an opportunity to apply the things you're learning and discussing in the group meetings and daily devotionals. They don't have to be done in any particular sequence, or on a particular day of the week. If you only have the physical or emotional energy to complete one of these exercises, that's fine. The point is to allow the Spirit of God to minister to your heart during this time of grief.

MAKING DECISIONS DURING A TIME OF GRIEF

Grief can make it difficult to think clearly about decisions big and small. A publication from Harvard Health explains that the fog of grief "can cloud thought processes, and people who make abrupt decisions may regret them later."[5]

These challenges make it all the more essential that we seek God's wisdom when making decisions during a time of grief.

One choice of wisdom can be to wait, if possible, for a year before making decisions with major ramifications. For example, these could include decisions to move into or out of a home, to change jobs or careers, to dispose of significant possessions, and so forth.

Of course, there are some decisions that have to be made on a more urgent basis. For instance, after a loved one's death, it may be necessary to deal in a timely way with matters related to funeral arrangements, insurance policies, vehicle and home titles, unpaid bills, etc. For these decisions, it's important to ask God for wisdom and, often, to ask other people for perspective and insight. God can use their input to help give you clarity.

As you work to process your grief, it may be helpful to keep a log of some of the decisions you're currently facing and categorize them into those that need to be dealt with now versus those that could be delayed for a time. Consider and write down your answers to the following questions:

- What major tasks or decisions do I feel pressing in on me now?

- Of these, which are truly urgent or time-sensitive matters that must be addressed in the near term? Which of these could be put off for later, perhaps even a year or more?

- Who can help me with these urgent tasks or decisions? Can any of them be delegated to someone else?

And one more question if you're having difficulty sorting through and categorizing these decisions: is there someone I can talk with about them—even someone to help me determine which decisions are urgent?

O **Action Item:** After recording your responses to these questions, take some time this week to discuss these matters with a trusted confidant—a pastor, a close friend, a family member. Can they provide any insight or helpful guidance as you navigate your way through these decisions?

ASSESSING YOUR CONDITION—PART ONE

The ultimate goal in everything the Lord allows into our lives is to grow us into spiritual maturity—into conformity with the image of His Son, Jesus Christ. As we've seen, though, it can be difficult for us to measure our growth, especially during times of grief, because our "gauges"—physical, mental, emotional, and spiritual—can be broken.

If we are to make healthy progress along the journey of grief, it will be helpful to know where we're starting from in order (eventually) to be able to see accurately the progress we've made on that road. In particular, it's helpful to assess where we currently are physically, mentally, emotionally, and spiritually. Starting with this session and continuing for the next few, we're going to take a look at each of these areas in turn. For this session, we'll consider how our grief is affecting us physically.

Take a few moments to think about and record your responses to the following questions:

- Am I sleeping well? Am I getting too much sleep? Too little?

- Am I getting enough to eat? Too much? Too little? Am I eating healthy foods that will nourish my body?

- Am I experiencing dizziness, headaches, or similar issues?

- Are my body's rhythms and cycles operating normally?

- Am I unusually tired, fatigued, or lethargic?

- Am I experiencing any other unusual physical symptoms or issues?

- Do I need help in any of these areas? If so, what kind of help do I need and who can I contact for assistance? For example, do I need to set up an appointment to see a doctor? To get a blood test?

If you have identified physical issues that may need attention, it's important to realize that it's okay to reach out for help. As we've seen in these first two lessons, grief is a long-term journey, not a short-term sprint—one doesn't just "shake it off' or "get over it" through sheer willpower. The road to healing can be a long one indeed, but along the way we are accompanied by our Heavenly Father, who knows our sorrows intimately, and by the people He has placed in our lives to minister His love to us.

O **Action Item:** If, after thinking about these questions, you've identified any areas in which you need assistance, make it a point to do something about it over the course of this next week. Do you need to set up an appointment to see a doctor? Talk to a pastor? Seek biblical counseling? Join a support group? Whatever it is, take at least one small step this week toward growing through your grief by caring for your physical, emotional, mental, and spiritual health.

STABILIZING YOUR SOUL

Using the words of a psalm or a biblically-saturated hymn or poem in prayer can be powerful medicine for your soul during this season of grief. When you can't come up with the words to say yourself, let others who have gone before you lead the way into the caring presence of your Father.

- **Action item:** Pray through these words of the well-known hymn "It is Well with my Soul." There is space provided after the hymn to record your reflections.

It is Well with My Soul
By Horatio Spafford

When peace like a river, attendeth my way,
When sorrows like sea billows roll;
Whatever my lot, Thou hast taught me to say
"It is well, it is well, with my soul."

Refrain

It is well, (it is well),
With my soul, (with my soul)
It is well, it is well, with my soul.

Though Satan should buffet, though trials should come,
Let this blest assurance control,
That Christ hath regarded my helpless estate,
And hath shed His own blood for my soul.

My sin, oh, the bliss of this glorious thought!
My sin, not in part but the whole,
Is nailed to His cross, and I bear it no more,
Praise the Lord, praise the Lord, O my soul!

For me, be it Christ, be it Christ hence to live:
If Jordan above me shall roll,
No pang shall be mine, for in death as in life,
Thou wilt whisper Thy peace to my soul.

But Lord, 'tis for Thee, for Thy coming we wait,
The sky, not the grave, is our goal;
Oh, trump of the angel! Oh, voice of the Lord!
Blessed hope, blessed rest of my soul.

And Lord, haste the day when my faith shall be sight,
The clouds be rolled back as a scroll;
The trump shall resound, and the Lord shall descend,
Even so, it is well with my soul.

BLESSED BE GOD, EVEN THE FATHER OF OUR LORD JESUS CHRIST, THE FATHER OF MERCIES, AND THE GOD OF ALL COMFORT; (2 CORINTHIANS 1:3)

RECEIVING GOD'S COMFORT

WHEN I AM HURTING

Session Notes

Discussion

Devotional Readings

1. Hope in God
2. Listening to the Voice of the Good Shepherd
3. The Power of Prayer
4. The Comfort of Others
5. New Every Morning

Personal Application

RECEIVING GOD'S COMFORT

"Blessed be God, even the Father of our Lord Jesus Christ, the Father of mercies, and the God of all comfort; 4 Who comforteth us in all our tribulation, that we may be able to comfort them which are in any trouble, by the comfort wherewith we ourselves are comforted of God. 5 For as the sufferings of Christ abound in us, so our consolation also aboundeth by Christ. 6 And whether we be afflicted, it is for your consolation and salvation, which is effectual in the enduring of the same sufferings which we also suffer: or whether we be comforted, it is for your consolation and salvation. 7 And our hope of you is stedfast, knowing, that as ye are partakers of the sufferings, so shall ye be also of the consolation." (2 Corinthians 1:3–7)

INTRODUCTION

____

____

____

"Blessed be God, even the Father of our Lord Jesus Christ, the Father of mercies, and the God of all comfort; 4 Who comforteth us in all our tribulation, that we may be able to comfort them which are in any trouble, by the comfort wherewith we ourselves are comforted of God." (2 Corinthians 1:3–4)

1. THE PERSON OF COMFORT

"Blessed be God, even the Father of our Lord Jesus Christ, the Father of mercies, and the God of all comfort; 4 Who comforteth us in all our tribulation ..." (2 Corinthians 1:3–4)

The Father of MERCIES

"It is of the LORD's mercies that we are not consumed, because his compassions fail not. 23 They are new every morning: great is thy faithfulness." (Lamentations 3:22–23)

The God of All COMFORT

"Now our Lord Jesus Christ himself, and God, even our Father, which hath loved us, and hath given us everlasting consolation and good hope through grace, 17 Comfort your hearts, and stablish you in every good word and work." (2 Thessalonians 2:16–17)

"I will not leave you comfortless: I will come to you." (John 14:18)

2. THE PROVISION OF COMFORT

"Who comforteth us in all our tribulation..." (2 Corinthians 1:4)

Definition: *Tribulation, from the Greek word thlipsis, "a pressing together, pressure; metaphorically oppression, affliction, distress."*

By His PRESENCE

"The LORD is nigh unto them that are of a broken heart; and saveth such as be of a contrite spirit." (Psalm 34:18)

"Yea, though I walk through the valley of the shadow of death, I will fear no evil: for thou art with me; thy rod and thy staff they comfort me." (Psalm 23:4)

"And I will pray the Father, and he shall give you another Comforter, that he may abide with you for ever; 17 Even the Spirit of truth; whom the world cannot receive, because it seeth him not, neither knoweth him: but ye know him; for he dwelleth with you, and shall be in you. 18 I will not leave you comfortless: I will come to you." (John 14:16–18)

By His WORK

"For whatsoever things were written aforetime were written for our learning, that we through patience and comfort of the scriptures might have hope." (Romans 15:4)

COMFORT FROM THE OLD TESTAMENT

1. ***Stories of Old Testament Believers***
2. ***Psalms***

   Unto thee, O Lord, do I lift up my soul. 2 O my God, I trust in thee: let me not be ashamed, let not mine enemies triumph over me. (Psalm 25:1–2)

   Hear my cry, O God; attend unto my prayer. 2 From the end of the earth will I cry unto thee, when my heart is overwhelmed: lead me to the rock that is higher than I. (Psalm 61:1–2)

   Trust in him at all times; ye people, pour out your heart before him: God is a refuge for us. Selah. (Psalm 62:8)

3. ***Pictures of Christ***

   Then he said unto them, O fools, and slow of heart to believe all that the prophets have spoken: 26 Ought not Christ to have suffered these things, and to enter into his glory? 27 And beginning at Moses and all the prophets, he expounded unto them in all the scriptures the things concerning himself. (Luke 24:25–27)

4. ***Promises***

By Others Who COME Alongside

"Nevertheless God, that comforteth those that are cast down, comforted us by the coming of Titus;" (2 Corinthians 7:6)

"And Jesus, which is called Justus, who are of the circumcision. These only are my fellowworkers unto the kingdom of God, which have been a comfort unto me." (Colossians 4:11)

"That is, that I may be comforted together with you by the mutual faith both of you and me." (Romans 1:12)

"That their hearts might be comforted, being knit together in love, and unto all riches of the full assurance of understanding, to the acknowledgement of the mystery of God, and of the Father, and of Christ;" (Colossians 2:2)

3. THE POWER OF COMFORT

"Who comforteth us in all our tribulation, that we may be able to comfort them which are in any trouble, by the comfort wherewith we ourselves are comforted of God. 5 For as the sufferings of Christ abound in us, so our consolation also aboundeth by Christ." (2 Corinthians 1:4–5)

"Rejoice with them that do rejoice, and weep with them that weep." (Romans 12:15)

ENDLESS Comfort

Definition: *Abound,* "to over flow, to be at hand in abundance."

"And he said unto me, My grace is sufficient for thee: for my strength is made perfect in weakness. Most gladly therefore will I rather glory in my infirmities, that the power of Christ may rest upon me." (2 Corinthians 12:9)

EFFECTIVE Comfort

"And whether we be afflicted, it is for your consolation and salvation, which is effectual in the enduring of the same sufferings which we also suffer: or whether we be comforted, it is for your consolation and salvation." (2 Corinthians 1:6)

Definition: *Afflicted,* from Greek *thlibo*, "to press (as grapes), pressure like being squeezed together.

FOR THE SALVATION OF OTHERS

"And the keeper of the prison awaking out of his sleep, and seeing the prison doors open, he drew out his sword, and would have killed himself, supposing that the prisoners had been fled.... 30 And brought them out, and said, Sirs, what must I do to be saved? 31 And they said, Believe on the Lord Jesus Christ, and thou shalt be saved, and thy house. 32 And they spake unto him the word of the Lord, and to all that were in his house. 33 And he took them the same hour of the night, and washed their stripes; and was baptized, he and all his, straightway." (Acts 16:27, 30–33)

FOR THE SANCTIFICATION OF OTHERS

"And our hope of you is stedfast, knowing, that as ye are partakers of the sufferings, so shall ye be also of the consolation." (2 Corinthians 1:7)

"Being confident of this very thing, that he which hath begun a good work in you will perform it until the day of Jesus Christ: 7 Even as it is meet for me to think this of you all, because I have you in my heart; inasmuch as both in my bonds, and in the defence and confirmation of the gospel, ye all are partakers of my grace." (Philippians 1:6–7)

"Who comforteth us in all our tribulation, that we may be able to comfort them which are in any trouble, by the comfort wherewith we ourselves are comforted of God." (2 Corinthians 1:4)

CONCLUSION

____

____

____

DISCUSSION

1. Was there anything from last week's devotionals or application exercises that was particularly meaningful or helpful to you? What passage of Scripture has been most reassuring to you this past week?

2. In those times when your grief has felt crushing, how has God brought comfort to you?

3. What have people said or done to comfort you that was helpful? What has perhaps been well-intentioned but unhelpful?

4. What is your favorite Psalm or verse from Psalms? What about it is comforting to you?

5. What is one way the group can pray for you as it relates to grief this week?

SESSION THREE: DAY ONE

HOPE IN GOD

My tears have been my meat day and night, while they continually say unto me, Where is thy God? When I remember these things, I pour out my soul in me: for I had gone with the multitude, I went with them to the house of God, with the voice of joy and praise, with a multitude that kept holyday. Why art thou cast down, O my soul? and why art thou disquieted in me? hope thou in God: for I shall yet praise him for the help of his countenance. (Psalm 42:3–5)

Abraham Lincoln and his wife Mary lost their second son Eddie in 1850 when he was just three years old. That same year their third son Willie was born. His parents doted on him as a replacement for their loss. During the Civil War when Lincoln was President, Willie fell sick, probably with typhoid fever, and in February 1862 died at the White House. The grief his parents felt was overwhelming. At one point Lincoln said, "I am now the most miserable man living. If what I feel was equally distributed to the whole human family, there would not be one cheerful face on the earth. Whether I shall ever be better, I cannot tell; I awfully forebode I shall not."

In those moments when it seems like there is no help to be found on Earth, those of us who know the Lord have another option. We can always look up. He never fails and never forgets His children. And when we look to Christ and saturate our hearts in His Word, we gain an eternal perspective that renews our spirits. It does not make our problems go away. But it enables us to see the larger reality of eternity. "For I reckon that the sufferings of this present time are not worthy to be compared with the glory which shall be revealed in us" (Romans 8:18).

In the times when all hope seems lost, we can remember the words of David in Psalm 42. In these verses, David talked to himself in the midst of his own season of grief and pain: "Why art thou cast down, O my soul? and why art thou disquieted in me?" (Psalm 42:5).

David had good reason to be distressed. Previously, he was able to go to the house of the Lord openly, worshipping God along with others (verse 4). Now, he found himself being mocked and taunted by his enemies (verses 3 and 10), crying continually (verse 3), suffering severe physical pain (verse 10), and—perhaps most agonizingly—longing to experience the Lord's presence intimately as he had in the past (verses 1–2). David's grief was real and palpable.

Yet, in the midst of the storm, David began speaking truth to his soul. He remembered the Lord's love for him, and a song arose—a "prayer unto the God of my life" (Psalm 42:8). Though it felt to David as if he were drowning, he had discovered that the Lord was with him (verse 7). David's fears, real as they were, could not stand in the face of the Lord's presence: "Hope thou in God: for I shall yet praise him," he concluded (Psalm 42:5, 11).

David was not alone in his grief, and neither are you. Hope in God. He is with you.

One day at a time, God will show you how to walk this road as well. You're not alone.

"And the LORD, he it is that doth go before thee; he will be with thee, he will not fail thee, neither forsake thee: fear not, neither be dismayed" (Deuteronomy 31:8).

"...he hath said, I will never leave thee, nor forsake thee" (Hebrews 13:5).

"And I will pray the Father, and he shall give you another Comforter, that he may abide with you for ever" (John 14:16).

TODAY'S TAKEAWAY

Whatever we face in life, God promises to remain with us.

JOURNAL PROMPT

What are some of the specific fears you're struggling with right now? For each fear you've listed, write one scriptural truth that can help bring calm and perspective to that fear. For example, if the fear is "I will never be happy again," the corresponding truth might be "weeping may endure for a night, but joy cometh in the morning" (Psalm 30:5)

Fear	Truth
____________________	____________________
____________________	____________________
____________________	____________________
____________________	____________________
____________________	____________________

SESSION THREE: DAY TWO

LISTENING TO THE VOICE OF THE GOOD SHEPHERD

The Lord is my shepherd; I shall not want. He maketh me to lie down in green pastures: he leadeth me beside the still waters. (Psalm. 23:1–2)

Psalm 23 is one of the most well-known and beloved passages of Scripture. Countless books, songs, and artistic works (not to mention a cottage industry of knickknacks and tchotchkes) have been inspired by this psalm. But what is it that makes it so enduring, so comforting to so many people?

Written by David—whose early years were spent as a shepherd—in simple, easily-understood language that employs vivid imagery, the psalm places the reader in the position of a sheep. David imagines himself (and by extension, the nation of Israel) as a sheep being guided by a good shepherd—the Lord Himself—who protects him, provides for his every need, and blesses him in unexpected ways.

As David knew from his own experience, a good shepherd will find places of safety, protection, and nourishment for his sheep to rest—the "green pastures" referred to in Psalm 23:1. He also knew another important fact about sheep: they're afraid of fast-moving water. With their heavy wool, sheep are not strong swimmers. If they try to drink water from a river or stream that is moving too quickly, there is a danger that they may fall in and drown. They need, instead, "still waters" (Psalm 23:2) from which to drink. A good shepherd knows this about his sheep and leads them to places where they will be able to find refreshment.

Grief, as we all know, can feel chaotic, fearful, and exhausting. But no matter how things may feel right now, we have a good Shepherd who is able to lead us to a place of peace and stillness. Even as we face uncertainty about the future, we don't have to become buried in the anxiety of questions like "what am I going to do now?" or "what is going to happen after . . . ?" We have a Shepherd who has a good and sovereign plan we can trust—even when we cannot yet see that plan.

In John 10 Jesus picked up the motif of this psalm and further developed it, identifying Himself as the "good shepherd" who "giveth his life for the sheep" (verse 11). The good shepherd doesn't just protect, provide for, and bless his sheep—he also sacrifices his own life to save them. He knows his sheep by name (verse 3), and they know Him and His voice (verses 4, 14). Having saved his sheep, the good shepherd keeps them secure forever: "I give unto them eternal life," Jesus says later in this chapter, "and they shall never perish, neither shall any man pluck them out of my hand. My Father, which gave them me, is greater than all; and no man is able to pluck them out of my Father's hand" (John 10:28–29).

For those of us going through a season of grief, these words can be a source of tremendous comfort. We have a Good Shepherd who is watching over us. And nothing—"neither death, nor life, nor angels, nor principalities, nor powers, nor things present, nor things to come, Nor height, nor depth, nor any other creature"—can separate us "from the love of God, which is in Christ Jesus our Lord" (Romans 8:38–39).

Thankfully, our Good Shepherd speaks to us today through His written Word, bringing peace and assurance through His promises. God uses His Word to comfort us during our times of grief. Let us draw near to our Good Shepherd and listen to His voice.

TODAY'S TAKEAWAY

We can find comfort in our time of grief by listening to the words of the Good Shepherd in the Word of God.

JOURNAL PROMPT

What Scripture verse or passage has God used in your life this past week to speak to you as His sheep?

SESSION THREE: DAY THREE

THE POWER OF PRAYER

Let us therefore come boldly unto the throne of grace, that we may obtain mercy, and find grace to help in time of need. (Hebrews 4:16)

The book of 1 Samuel begins with the story of Hannah and her long struggle with infertility. For many years, Hannah looked on as her rival wife, Peninnah, bore children to their shared husband Elkanah. The grief of infertility was made even more painful by the fact that Peninnah continually taunted Hannah over her barrenness. Hannah's distress was so profound that she wept and refused to eat. Her husband, while sympathetic, couldn't understand the anguish in her heart: "Hannah, why weepest thou? and why eatest thou not? and why is thy heart grieved? am not I better to thee than ten sons?" (verse 8). Often, even those who love us the most cannot fully enter into our grief and pain. By its very nature, grief isolates.

So, year after year, Hannah prayed—and year after year, her heart and home remained empty: no children, and seemingly no hope for the future. One year, while the family was at the temple for their annual sacrifice to the Lord, Hannah "was in bitterness of soul, and prayed unto the LORD, and wept sore" (verse 10). Perhaps in desperation, she made a vow to the Lord: "if thou wilt indeed look on the affliction of thine handmaid, and remember me, and not forget thine handmaid, but wilt give unto thine handmaid a man child, then I will give him unto the LORD all the days of his life" (verse 11). Eli the high priest saw her praying silently but with lips moving and mistook her fervor for drunkenness (verses 13–14). To Eli's rebuke, Hannah responded, "No, my Lord, I am a woman of a sorrowful spirit: I have drunk neither wine nor strong drink, but have poured out my soul before the LORD" (verse15). Realizing his mistake, Eli pronounced a blessing on Hannah: "go in peace: and the God of Israel grant thee thy petition that thou hast asked of him" (verse 17).

This time, Hannah returned home feeling encouraged; she ate food, and "her countenance was no more sad" (verse 18). Shortly thereafter, she became pregnant and gave birth to a son, whom she and her husband named Samuel.

Hannah later fulfilled her vow to the Lord by dedicating Samuel to the Lord's service in the temple (verses 24–28). In her season of grief and despair, the Lord had heard her prayer. And, looking back on God's faithfulness to her, Hannah could now proclaim, "My heart rejoiceth in the LORD, mine horn is exalted in the LORD: my mouth is enlarged over mine enemies; because I rejoice in thy salvation" (1 Samuel 2:1). Hannah's season of grief had not been in vain—and it had now turned to joy.

Prayer is not a "vending machine" from which we automatically get what we want from the Lord. But it is our gateway into His loving presence. Therefore, "let us . . . come boldly unto the throne of grace, that we may obtain mercy, and find grace to help in time of need" (Hebrews 4:16). Like Hannah, we can pour out our hearts to him, even in the "abundance of [our] complaint and grief" (1 Samuel 1:16). And we can rest assured that He hears our prayers.

God comforts us through prayer. Let us not underestimate its power.

TODAY'S TAKEAWAY

When we pour out our hearts to the Lord in prayer, He hears and comforts us in the midst of our grief and pain.

JOURNAL PROMPT

What do you want to ask the Lord for during this time of grief? Write down your requests here. Don't be afraid to approach His throne of grace with boldness; He loves you and wants to hear from you as you pour your heart out to Him.

SESSION THREE: DAY FOUR

THE COMFORT OF OTHERS

Who comforteth us in all our tribulation, that we may be able to comfort them which are in any trouble, by the comfort wherewith we ourselves are comforted of God. (2 Corinthians 1:4)

In yesterday's devotional, we looked at the story of Hannah, whose struggle with infertility was a source of profound grief for many years. In the end, God blessed Hannah with the birth of Samuel, who would later become a prophet of the Lord and a leader of His people.

Of course, not every story ends this way.

Consider the case of Laura, a Christian woman who married late in life. Like many women, one of Laura's earliest dreams in life was to be a mother. Within a year of marriage, she became pregnant but shortly thereafter had a miscarriage before she'd had time to tell anyone that she was pregnant. For two years, she carried the burden of grief alone. During that time, she was almost always on the verge of tears—without knowing or understanding why. She chalked the fear and anxiety she was feeling up to the stress of a long work commute, financial pressures, and the other challenges of everyday life.

One day, as she was surrounded by friends in a time of prayer, the Lord mercifully revealed to her the grief and trauma she had suppressed. After two years of suffering in silence, Laura was able to share her grief with her friends, who then prayed with and for her. That simple yet powerful moment was the beginning of healing for Laura.

Sometimes God answers our prayer in grief with exactly what we ask for; other times, He gives us something we didn't even know we needed. But His comfort and healing are always available, and receiving them begins with coming to Him in prayer. Laura, surrounded by her fellow believers, prayed for the gift of healing from her trauma, and now she is able to encourage others with the comfort she has received from the Lord.

But note this: God's comfort came, in part, *through* the loving presence of Laura's friends, who took the time to be with and pray for her. There is an aspect of healing that God often brings in the context of community. Community can come in various forms, including a church family and support groups like this one. Rest assured that your very presence in this group is a gift and a blessing to the other members.

God brings comfort to us through the ministry of others, and He uses us to bring His comfort to others as well. These realities should encourage us to fight the tendency toward isolating ourselves in grief.

TODAY'S TAKEAWAY

God ministers to us in our grief through the comfort of other believers who come alongside us in prayer and fellowship.

JOURNAL PROMPT

Who has God brought alongside you on this journey of grief—people to whom you can turn for prayer, fellowship, and comfort? Take a moment to thank God for them and to pray for them.

SESSION THREE: DAY FIVE

NEW EVERY MORNING

This I recall to my mind, therefore have I hope. It is of the LORD's mercies that we are not consumed, because his compassions fail not. They are new every morning: great is thy faithfulness. (Lamentations 3:21–23)

In 1923, a minister named Thomas O. Chisholm was meditating on the words of Lamentations 3:22–23 and wrote a poem based on them. The result was the lyrics to the beloved hymn "Great Is Thy Faithfulness," which were later put to music by fellow minister William Runyan. Though Chisholm lived, by all accounts, "a pretty unremarkable life," and although the writing of this poem was not occasioned by any particularly heart-wrenching circumstances (as was the case, for example, with Horatio Spafford's song "It is Well with My Soul"), Chisholm was not immune to the difficulties and hardships of life.[1]

Chisholm suffered over the course of his life from various health challenges, and, apparently as a result, struggled financially as well. Still, he wrote, "I must not fail to record here the unfailing faithfulness of a covenant-keeping God and that He has given me many wonderful displays of His providing care, for which I am filled with astonishing gratefulness."[2] What Chisholm was able to see—and what he recorded in a form that would bless generations of believers after him—was the reality of a faithful God who shows up with mercy in the ordinary details of everyday life.

Scripture provides a clear-eyed perspective about the hard realities of life in a fallen world. Space is given for God's people to express their grief, sorrow, questions, and even anger over their experiences of loss and hardship. In fact, an entire book of the Bible is devoted to recording a series of laments over the destruction (in 586 B.C.) of the city of Jerusalem and the devastation of the nation of Judah by the Babylonians.

Over the millennia since the words of Lamentations were originally penned, God's people have continued to find Him faithful and reliable day in and day out, in the ordinary and extraordinary times, in times of hardship and in times of ease.

God's mercies can be seen in a sunrise or sunset, the smile and laughter of your grandchild playing in the park, and the warm embrace of your brother or sister in Christ with whom you worship at church. May we, like Chisholm and so many others who have gone before us, have eyes to see and ears to hear Him at work (Matthew 13:9–17).

TODAY'S TAKEAWAY

In a million different ways, large and small, God pours out His mercies upon us every day.

JOURNAL PROMPT

Yesterday or today may have been excruciatingly painful for you, but with each new day comes new hope because of the mercies of God. Look for these "new mercies" that God puts into your life on a daily basis—and allow them to fuel your confidence in a God whose faithfulness can give you hope for your future.

What is one "new mercy" that God has shown to you in the past twenty-four hours? Record it here and spend some time thanking God for His faithfulness.

PERSONAL APPLICATION

The following exercises are intended to give you an opportunity to apply the things you're learning and discussing in the group meetings and daily devotionals. They don't have to be done in any particular sequence, or on a particular day of the week. If you only have the physical or emotional energy to complete one of these exercises, that's fine. The point is to allow the Spirit of God to minister to your heart during this time of grief.

FINDING COMFORT ALONG THE JOURNEY

As we've seen in this lesson, God provides comfort through His presence, His Word, and through the people He places in our lives to walk alongside us. He can also use things like music, art, poetry, the beauty of nature, and a host of other daily mercies to comfort our hurting hearts.

What are the things that God uses to minister His grace to your soul? Time spent with a friend or family member over a warm cup of coffee? Time spent in prayer or meditation on His Word? Something else? Take some time to list a few things that come to mind.

Now, think about how you might incorporate at least one of these into your life this week. For example, if music is one of the means that God uses to comfort you, why not compile a playlist of your favorite songs? Then, work your way through that playlist as you go throughout this next week. Let the music you listen to express the prayer of your heart in the days to come.

○ **Action Item:** Plan a time to incorporate at least one item from the list you've created into your life over the course of this week.

ASSESSING YOUR CONDITION—PART TWO

In the last session's application exercises, we took a look at our physical status; this week, we'll consider how our grief is affecting our mental state.

Grief, especially when it is prolonged, can have significant impacts on cognitive functioning. Among other effects, "grief can disrupt the diverse cognitive domains of memory, decision-making, visuospatial function, attention, word fluency, and the speed of information processing." This has to do in part with the fact that the human brain "interprets grief as emotional trauma." In response to this perceived trauma, the "fight or flight" mechanism is engaged, which can involve increased blood pressure and heart rate, as well as elevated levels of various hormones. In short, grief and loss can impact the brain and body in a variety of ways, including "changes in memory, behavior, sleep, and body function, affecting the immune system as well as the heart. [They] can also lead to cognitive effects, such as brain fog."[3]

The good news is that these are normal effects of the grieving process, and healing comes with time. In some instances, though, the grieving person may need to seek medical or other assistance to help them get back on track with the healing process.

Take a few moments to think about and record your responses to the following questions:

Questions regarding my cognitive functions:

- Am I having trouble remembering things?

____

____

- Am I having trouble connecting my thoughts?

- Am I having difficulty making decisions?

- Are my thoughts confused?

- Do I need to seek medical attention, counseling, or other assistance to help me deal with any mental/cognitive issues I am experiencing? If so, what kind of assistance do I need and from whom do I need to seek it?

It's important to reiterate that when you're dealing with grief, it is normal to experience some degree of difficulty in connecting your thoughts or remembering things. If you're having a hard time with this, rest assured that you are experiencing what most people experience when they go through grief.

○ **Action Item:** If, after thinking about these questions, you've identified any areas in which you need assistance, make it a point to do something about it over the course of this next week. Do you need to set up an appointment to see a doctor? Talk to a pastor? Seek biblical counseling? Join a support group? Whatever it is, take at least one small step this week toward growing through your grief by caring for your physical, emotional, mental, and spiritual health.

STABILIZING YOUR SOUL

The pages of Scripture—both the Old and the New Testament—are replete with God's promises. Those promises reveal to us who God is and what He offers to us during our season of grief. One way of stabilizing our souls in the midst of our grief, then, is to meditate on the promises of God's Word and keep them in the forefront of our minds as we go throughout our day-to-day lives. This exercise is intended to help you do that.

- [ ] **Action item:** Take a look at the list of "God's Promises for Grieving Christians" provided at the end of this book. From that list, pick five passages that you find particularly meaningful. Over this next week, pick one of these passages per day (for five days) on which to meditate. Write out the text of each verse and summarize the promise in your own words in the space provided here. As you go along, make note of any insights or special words of comfort that the Lord provides during these times of meditation.

1. **Promise #1**

   Scripture:

   What this verse promises to me:

2. **Promise #2**

   Scripture:

   ___

   ___

   What this verse promises to me:

   ___

   ___

3. **Promise #3**

   Scripture:

   ___

   ___

   What this verse promises to me:

   ___

   ___

4. **Promise #4**

   Scripture:

   ____

   ____

   What this verse promises to me:

   ____

   ____

5. **Promise #5**

   Scripture:

   ____

   ____

   What this verse promises to me:

   ____

   ____

FOR I KNOW THE THOUGHTS THAT I THINK TOWARD YOU, SAITH THE LORD, THOUGHTS OF PEACE, AND NOT OF EVIL, TO GIVE YOU AN EXPECTED END. (JEREMIAH 29:11)

RESTING IN GOD'S GOODNESS

WHEN I QUESTION GOD

Session Notes

Discussion

Devotional Readings

1. Through a Glass, Darkly
2. In the Father's Embrace
3. Trusting God's Promises
4. Fighting Despair
5. Footprints

Personal Application

RESTING IN GOD'S GOODNESS

"When Mordecai perceived all that was done, Mordecai rent his clothes, and put on sackcloth with ashes, and went out into the midst of the city, and cried with a loud and a bitter cry; 2 And came even before the king's gate: for none might enter into the king's gate clothed with sackcloth. 3 And in every province, whithersoever the king's commandment and his decree came, there was great mourning among the Jews, and fasting, and weeping, and wailing; and many lay in sackcloth and ashes. 4 So Esther's maids and her chamberlains came and told it her. Then was the queen exceedingly grieved; and she sent raiment to clothe Mordecai, and to take away his sackcloth from him: but he received it not. 5 Then called Esther for Hatach, one of the king's chamberlains, whom he had appointed to attend upon her, and gave him a commandment to Mordecai, to know what it was, and why it was. 6 So Hatach went forth to Mordecai unto the street of the city, which was before the king's gate. 7 And Mordecai told him of all that had happened unto him, and of the sum of the money that Haman had promised to pay to the king's treasuries for the Jews, to destroy them. 8 Also he gave him the copy of the writing of the decree that was given at Shushan to destroy them, to shew it unto Esther, and to declare it unto her, and to charge her that she should go in unto the king, to make supplication unto him, and to make request before him for her people. 9 And Hatach came and told Esther the words of Mordecai. 10 Again Esther spake unto Hatach, and gave him commandment unto Mordecai; 11 All the king's servants, and the people of the king's provinces, do know, that whosoever, whether man or women, shall come unto the king into the inner court, who is not called, there is one law of his to put him to death, except such to whom the king shall hold out the golden sceptre, that he may live: but I have not been called to come in unto the king these thirty days. 12 And they told to Mordecai Esther's words. 13 Then Mordecai commanded to answer Esther, Think not with thyself that thou shalt escape in the king's house, more than all the Jews. 14 For if thou altogether holdest thy peace at this time, then shall there enlargement and deliverance arise to the Jews from another place; but thou and thy father's house shall be destroyed: and who knoweth whether thou art come to the kingdom for such a time as this? 15 Then Esther bade them return Mordecai this answer, 16 Go, gather together all the Jews that are present in Shushan, and fast ye for me, and neither eat nor drink three days, night or day: I also and my maidens will fast likewise; and so will I go in unto the king, which is not according to the law: and if I perish, I perish. 17 So Mordecai went his way, and did according to all that Esther had commanded him." (Esther 4:1–17)

INTRODUCTION

"*For I know the thoughts that I think toward you, saith the* L*ORD, thoughts of peace, and not of evil, to give you an expected end.*" (Jeremiah 29:11)

Definition: *Sovereign*—"Supreme ruler." This can be a king, queen, or emperor. As it relates to God, it refers to the fact that He is *the* Sovereign—He is the supreme ruler and is in control of this world.

Definition: *Goodness*—"the state or quality of being good. Moral excellence or virtue." As it relates to God, this means that everything He does is right and good.

1. GOD IS IN control

"*Remember the former things of old: for I am God, and there is none else; I am God, and there is none like me, 10 Declaring the end from the beginning, and from ancient times the things that are not yet done, saying, My counsel shall stand, and I will do all my pleasure:*" (Isaiah 46:9–10)

"*Ah Lord GOD! behold, thou hast made the heaven and the earth by thy great power and stretched out arm, and there is nothing too hard for thee:*" (Jeremiah 32:17)

"*My help cometh from the* L*ORD, which made heaven and earth.*" (Psalm 121:2)

He Is powerful

"*And he brought up Hadassah, that is, Esther, his uncle's daughter: for she had neither father nor mother, and the maid was fair and beautiful; whom Mordecai, when her father and mother were dead, took for his own daughter.*" (Esther 2:7)

"*Then said the king's servants that ministered unto him, Let there be fair young virgins sought for the king: 3 And let the king appoint officers in all the provinces of his kingdom, that they may gather together all the fair young virgins unto Shushan the palace, to the house of the women, unto the custody of Hege the king's chamberlain, keeper of the women; and let their things for purification be given them: 4 And let the maiden which pleaseth the king be queen instead of Vashti. And the thing pleased the king; and he did so.*" (Esther 2:2–4)

"And the king loved Esther above all the women, and she obtained grace and favour in his sight more than all the virgins; so that he set the royal crown upon her head, and made her queen instead of Vashti." (Esther 2:17)

"Esther had not yet shewed her kindred nor her people; as Mordecai had charged her: for Esther did the commandment of Mordecai, like as when she was brought up with him." (Esther 2:20)

"If it please the king, let it be written that they may be destroyed: and I will pay ten thousand talents of silver to the hands of those that have the charge of the business, to bring it into the king's treasuries. 10 And the king took his ring from his hand, and gave it unto Haman the son of Hammedatha the Agagite, the Jews' enemy. 11 And the king said unto Haman, The silver is given to thee, the people also, to do with them as it seemeth good to thee." (Esther 3:9–11)

"When Mordecai perceived all that was done, Mordecai rent his clothes, and put on sackcloth with ashes, and went out into the midst of the city, and cried with a loud and a bitter cry;" (Esther 4:1)

"Thine, O LORD, is the greatness, and the power, and the glory, and the victory, and the majesty: for all that is in the heaven and in the earth is thine; thine is the kingdom, O LORD, and thou art exalted as head above all. 12 Both riches and honour come of thee, and thou reignest over all; and in thine hand is power and might; and in thine hand it is to make great, and to give strength unto all." (1 Chronicles 29:11– 12)

"The LORD reigneth, he is clothed with majesty; the LORD is clothed with strength, wherewith he hath girded himself: the world also is stablished, that it cannot be moved. 2 Thy throne is established of old: thou art from everlasting." (Psalm 93:1–2)

"The LORD hath prepared his throne in the heavens; and his kingdom ruleth over all." (Psalm 103:19)

He Is good

"The LORD is good to all: and his tender mercies are over all his works." (Psalm 145:9)

"For the LORD is good; his mercy is everlasting; and his truth endureth to all generations." (Psalm 100:5)

"The LORD is good unto them that wait for him, to the soul that seeketh him." (Lamentations 3:25)

Quote: *All of our trials are Father-filtered.*

"The LORD is good, a strong hold in the day of trouble; and he knoweth them that trust in him." (Nahum 1:7)

"Thou art good, and doest good; teach me thy statutes." (Psalm 119:68)

2. GOD IS working BEHIND THE SCENES

Quote: *"While there is no name of God, and no mention of the Hebrew religion anywhere, no one reads this book without being conscious of God."* **—G. Campbell Morgan**

Quote: *"If the name of God is not here, His finger is."*—**Matthew Henry**

Quote: *"Providence is God's attention concentrated everywhere.* **— Augustus Strong**

"The eyes of all wait upon thee; and thou givest them their meat in due season.
16 Thou openest thine hand, and satisfiest the desire of every living thing."
(Psalm 145:15–16)

Quote: *"The sovereignty of God is often questioned because man does not understand what God is doing. Because He does not act as we think He should, we conclude He cannot act as we think He would."*—**Jerry Bridges**

"For my thoughts are not your thoughts, neither are your ways my ways, saith the
LORD. 9 For as the heavens are higher than the earth, so are my ways higher than
your ways, and my thoughts than your thoughts." (Isaiah 55:8–9)

"For I reckon that the sufferings of this present time are not worthy to be compared with the glory which shall be revealed in us." (Romans 8:18)

3. GOD HAS A PURPOSE FOR YOU IN THIS MOMENT

"*When Mordecai perceived all that was done, Mordecai rent his clothes, and put on sackcloth with ashes, and went out into the midst of the city, and cried with a loud and a bitter cry; 2 And came even before the king's gate: for none might enter into the king's gate clothed with sackcloth. 3 And in every province, whithersoever the king's commandment and his decree came, there was great mourning among the Jews, and fasting, and weeping, and wailing; and many lay in sackcloth and ashes." (Esther 4:1–3)*

Reject DESPAIR

"*How long wilt thou forget me, O LORD? for ever? how long wilt thou hide thy face from me?... 5 But I have trusted in thy mercy; my heart shall rejoice in thy salvation. 6 I will sing unto the LORD, because he hath dealt bountifully with me." (Psalm 13:1, 5–6)*

Walk foward in FAITH

"*All the king's servants, and the people of the king's provinces, do know, that whosoever, whether man or woman, shall come unto the king into the inner court, who is not called, there is one law of his to put him to death, except such to whom the king shall hold out the golden sceptre, that he may live: but I have not been called to come in unto the king these thirty days." (Esther 4:11)*

"*Then Mordecai commanded to answer Esther, Think not with thyself that thou shalt escape in the king's house, more than all the Jews. 14 For if thou altogether holdest thy peace at this time, then shall there enlargement and deliverance arise to the Jews from another place; but thou and thy father's house shall be destroyed: and who knoweth whether thou art come to the kingdom for such a time as this?" (Esther 4:13–14)*

"*Go, gather together all the Jews that are present in Shushan, and fast ye for me, and neither eat nor drink three days, night or day: I also and my maidens will fast likewise; and so will I go in unto the king, which is not according to the law: and if I perish, I perish." (Esther 4:16)*

"*Therefore we are always confident, knowing that, whilst we are at home in the body, we are absent from the Lord: 7 (For we walk by faith, not by sight:)" (2 Corinthians 5:6–7)*

THREE STEPS OF FAITH EVERY GRIEF-STRICKEN CHRISTIAN CAN TAKE

1. ***Praise God for who He is.***

   "Why art thou cast down, O my soul? and why art thou disquieted within me? hope thou in God: for I shall yet praise him, who is the health of my countenance, and my God." (Psalm 42:11)

2. ***Pour your heart out to God.***

   "Trust in him at all times; ye people, pour out your heart before him: God is a refuge for us. Selah." (Psalm 62:8)

3. ***Persist in regular worship.***

   "But without faith it is impossible to please him: for he that cometh to God must believe that he is, and that he is a rewarder of them that diligently seek him." (Hebrews 11:6)

CONCLUSION

DISCUSSION

1. Was there anything from last week's devotionals or application exercises that was particularly meaningful or helpful to you? What passage of Scripture has been most reassuring to you this past week?

2. What are three ways in which God has shown His goodness to you over the years? In what ways can you look back over this past week and see God's goodness?

3. How does remembering the reality of God's sovereignty bring comfort in grief?

4. What are a few differences between grief and despair? How can you tell if your grief is turning (has turned) into despair?

5. What is one way the group can pray for you as it relates to grief this week? (Space is provided at the end of the book for you to record the requests of other group members.)

SESSION FOUR: DAY ONE

THROUGH A GLASS, DARKLY

For now we see through a glass, darkly; but then face to face: now I know in part; but then shall I know even as also I am known. (1 Corinthians 13:12)

If you've ever driven a car in a heavy thunderstorm, you know how difficult it can be to see where you are going. Fortunately, we can usually see just enough of what's ahead of us—road signs, streetlights, other vehicles, etc.—to keep us safe.

When grief enters our lives, our vision can become cloudy—much like looking through the windshield of a car in the midst of a violent downpour or trying to see through a darkened window. It can be difficult to see the way ahead of us or even to fully discern the circumstances surrounding us.

The reality is that not just in grief—but in all of life this side of Heaven—we don't have the full perspective. As 1 Corinthians 13:12 observes, we can only "see through a glass, darkly."

Thankfully, however, there's good news: there is more to the story than our clouded vision. First, we can rejoice in knowing that even though we cannot clearly see God, He sees us. We are, right now, in this very moment, fully known by God.

Second, we can rejoice in knowing that there is coming a day when every tear that obscures our vision now will be wiped away and we will see Christ face to face. First John 3:2 tells us that when Christ appears, "we shall be like him; for we shall see him as he is." This is good news indeed, for it means that even though we aren't always able to understand God or His ways now, there will be a glorious day when we stand face to face with Jesus—and we will understand everything we could ever need to know.

We may not know exactly what it will be like when we see Christ (we may not know a lot of things!), but we can rest assured that in that moment we will be like Him and understand Him, because we will finally see Him.

In the meantime, though, as we look through tear-filled eyes, we can see the form of our loving Father who walks with us through the storm. If we keep our eyes on Him, we will find our way—even if we don't find all the answers to our questions.

TODAY'S TAKEAWAY

We can find comfort today in knowing that a glorious day is coming when we will know and understand all of God's purposes—and that, in the meantime, we are fully known and fully loved by Him.

JOURNAL PROMPT

What are some of the questions you would ask God if you could see Him today? Write them down here. Then, take a moment to thank God that you are known and ask Him for the grace and forbearance that you need when you struggle with what you cannot know this side of eternity.

SESSION FOUR: DAY TWO

IN THE FATHER'S EMBRACE

For I know the thoughts that I think toward you, saith the LORD, thoughts of peace, and not of evil, to give you an expected end. (Jeremiah 29:11)

The words of Jeremiah 29:11 were written to the people of God suffering in exile. They had experienced the horror of seeing their homeland destroyed and their people slaughtered. They were a grieving people who desperately needed hope. God, who knows our need for hope better than we do, sent a message to reaffirm His people that His intentions and plans for them were good and that He had a good "expected end" for them in mind. He was preparing a future of return from exile and renewed fellowship with Himself.

Previously, God made a covenant with the Israelites that the Messiah would come from them and that through the Messiah peace with God would be offered to the world. Now, God reassured them that even though they were suffering at the hands of others and as a consequence of their own sin, His plan had not changed. He had not forgotten His promises to His people.

Unfortunately, sin and suffering often live side by side—whether that be because of the specific consequences of sin-driven tragedies such as addiction, abandonment, or abuse, or the general consequences of human sinfulness, including death itself. We live in a fallen world that is full of heartache and pain. Sometimes we simply can't "make peace" with our circumstances. And yet, we can be at peace with God through faith in Christ (Romans 5:1–2) and have the peace of God (Philippians 4:7).

Your faith in Christ for salvation, and your faith that He is good and will only be good to you, will give you the strength you need to expect goodness for today and for your future. God did not forget about the Israelites in captivity; He has not forgotten about you either.

God's plan for us is that we would experience peace with Him, even as we undergo painful circumstances. As Jeremiah 29:11 reminds us, He is not creating a plan that is against us or intended to destroy us. He loves us. Our hope is found in Him today as we grieve and tomorrow as we heal. He holds our future, and it is good—because it is with Him.

Pain in any variety—whether physical, emotional, or spiritual—is never pleasant. But we can experience God's blessing in the midst of the pain when we allow it to press us into the embrace of our loving Father who holds us in His arms. We can trust Him when He tells us that His plans for us are good and that we can have hope for the future even in the midst of present pain and grief.

TODAY'S TAKEAWAY

Because our Father's intentions toward us are good, we can have hope for our future even in the midst of present pain and grief.

JOURNAL PROMPT

How is your future different now than what you had hoped for? Share with the Lord those aspects of your future that you need to grieve because they are now (or seem) foreclosed. Based on the character of God, write down how you know that you can still have hope for your future.

SESSION FOUR: DAY THREE

TRUSTING GOD'S PROMISES

And he believed in the LORD; and he counted it to him for righteousness. (Genesis 15:6)

When we think of Abraham, we tend to think of faith. After all, he is known as "the father of faith" (see Galatians 3:6–7) and is a central figure in the so-called "Faith Hall of Fame" recorded in Hebrews 11.

One word we don't always associate with Abraham, though, is grief. But when we take a closer look at Abraham's life, we quickly realize that it was punctuated by seasons of profound grief.

While he was still named Abram, God called him to leave everything behind—his relatives, his wealth and possessions, his people and culture, his reputation and status—all the things that would have given him a sense of identity. Though Abram went in response to the Lord's call and with His promise that He would bless him and make him into a "great nation" (Genesis 12:2–3), one can only imagine that Abram grieved the loss of the life and relationships he had known up to that point.

Later, the Lord added greater detail to His promise: Abram (later to be renamed Abraham) would have a son who would be his heir, and his descendants would be more numerous than the stars in the sky (Genesis 15:4–5). No doubt this seemed utterly impossible to Abram—after all, Sarai's womb had been barren up to that point, and neither of them were getting any younger. Nevertheless, Abram "believed in the LORD; and he counted it to him for righteousness" (Genesis 15:6).

Still later, when the child of the promise, Isaac, had finally arrived after decades of waiting, God asked Abraham to sacrifice his son on an altar on Mount Moriah. Imagine the grief Abraham must have felt as he and his son trudged toward that mountain, step by step, anticipating with increasing dread the deed he would have to perform once he reached their destination. True, Abraham answered Isaac's question about the absence of a lamb by saying that the Lord would provide a sacrifice for them (Genesis 22:8).

And, yes, Abraham reasoned "that God was able to raise him up, even from the dead" (Hebrews 11:19). Still, Abraham was a father—and no good father can imagine doing what God had asked him to do. No doubt the weight of grief grew stronger with each step they took.

Ultimately, faith is about trust. Abraham was able to keep putting one foot in front of the other—all the way to Mount Moriah—because he knew he could trust God's promises. He could trust God's promises because he knew God's character. And that, in turn, gave him what he needed to be able to climb the mountain prepared to give up the very fulfillment of the promise that God had made to him.

Sometimes God asks us to be willing to give up the most precious thing in our lives. And that may cause us grief. But even in the midst of that grief, we can trust that He will always fulfill His promises to us—even if it's not in the way we had hoped or expected.

TODAY'S TAKEAWAY

In the midst of our grief, we can trust that God will always fulfill His promises to us—even if it's not in the way we had hoped or expected.

JOURNAL PROMPT

Make a written declaration of things you know to be true about God's nature—who He is and what He does—that can help you trust His promises. Here are a few examples to get you started:

- He is near to me. (Psalm 145:18)
- He is giving me mercy and grace in my time of need. (Hebrews 4:16)
- I am an amazing work of God, with a God-given purpose. (Ephesians 2:10)

SESSION FOUR: DAY FOUR

FIGHTING DESPAIR

How long wilt thou forget me, O Lord? (Psalm 13:1)

On one of the numerous occasions when David faced the very real prospect of death, he found himself feeling abandoned and forgotten by God. Undeterred, he took his complaints directly to the Lord: "How long wilt thou forget me, O Lord? for ever? how long wilt thou hide thy face from me?"

Then, through the next few verses of Psalm 13, David listed his troubles—and they are troubles familiar to those experiencing grief: I can't stop my mind from racing, and my heart is overwhelmed with sorrow (verse 2). My enemy is winning over me, and if I die—as seems likely—he will claim victory and others will rejoice (verses 2–4). Things are looking bleak, and time is running out (verse 3).

But then, David intentionally turned his attention to God's character: despite all that was happening to him, David said, "I have trusted in thy mercy" (verse 5). As a result, he could rejoice and even sing (verses 5–6).

This pattern repeats itself over and over in the psalms. In Psalm 77:7–9, for example, Asaph inquires, "Will the Lord cast off for ever? and will he be favourable no more? Is his mercy clean gone for ever? doth his promise fail for evermore? Hath God forgotten to be gracious? hath he in anger shut up his tender mercies?" But then, he turns his attention to remembering what the Lord has done in the past, from which he derives hope for the future: "And I said, This is my infirmity: but I will remember the years of the right hand of the most High. I will remember the works of the Lord: surely I will remember thy wonders of old. I will meditate also of all thy work, and talk of thy doings" (Psalm 77:10–12).

The psalms give us ways to talk honestly with God, expressing the wide range of emotions we're feeling—anger, sadness, abandonment, and rejection, as well as joy, happiness, and hope. No matter what stage of grief we might happen to find ourselves in, there is a psalm fit for that moment. They connect with every emotion we might feel—anger, denial, depression, and so much more. And they provide us with healthy ways of channeling those emotions—to God, our only true source of help in time of need—and, thereby, of staving off despair.

Despair says things like "I have no hope," "God has abandoned me," "I will always be a victim," "Nothing will ever change," and, finally, "It's no use—I'm giving up."

The key to fighting despair is to remember what the Lord has done for us and others in the past, to trust in His unchanging character, and to rest on His promises for the future.

When we pour out our grief to God honestly, we can be sure that He cares. Why? Because He too grieves over the pain, heartache, and sorrow that characterizes human existence this side of eternity. Jesus Himself was "a man of sorrows, and acquainted with grief" (Isaiah 53:3). And God has promised that, someday, He will wipe away every tear from our eyes (Revelation 21:4).

TODAY'S TAKEAWAY

When we pour out our grief to God, we can rest assured that He cares because He grieves with us. Reminding ourselves of this fact—and the fact that God has a plan to restore a fallen, broken world—can give us hope for the future and serve as a bulwark against despair.

JOURNAL PROMPT

Despair lies to us. Take a few minutes to write down some of the lies of despair—perhaps ones that have crossed your own mind or ones that you know of in general. Then, ask, "What truth from God's Word answers and contradicts this lie?" Write that truth in the right column. Consider coming back to this list over the next few days to add truths and specific Scripture references as they come to mind.

Lie of Despair	Truth of God's Word

SESSION FOUR: DAY FIVE

FOOTPRINTS

The Lord is nigh unto them that are of a broken heart; and saveth such as be of a contrite spirit. (Psalm 34:18)

There is a poem, well-known in Christian circles, called "Footprints in the Sand." It has found its way onto countless coffee mugs, paintings, and other Christian-themed memorabilia. Its original authorship is disputed and there are multiple versions of the poem in existence, with slightly different wording in each case. Regardless of the version, though, the basic premise and underlying themes of the poem remain the same. Narrated by an individual who is looking back over the course of her life, the poem recounts a conversation she had with the Lord as they walked together along a sandy beach.

As scenes from the narrator's life unfold, corresponding sets of footprints appear in the sand. Frequently there are two sets of footprints, but disturbingly, the narrator notices that only one set accompanies those scenes from her life that represent her hardest and darkest seasons. She asks God why He apparently wasn't with her during those times. In response, He says that those were the times when He was actually carrying her. She realizes then that He didn't forsake her in her hard times; He held her tenderly.

When the nation of Israel was about to enter the promised land after forty years of wandering in the wilderness, Moses made a point of reminding the people that the Lord Himself had carried them, "as a man doth bear his son, in all the way that ye went, until ye came into this place" (Deuteronomy 1:31).

Jesus tells us that He is the "good shepherd" who "giveth his life for the sheep" (John 10:11). On occasion a shepherd will actually carry a sheep under his care, particularly if that sheep is injured. This is how Jesus cares for us when we are weighed down by grief and sadness.

Even when we can't plainly sense the Lord's presence with us, we can rest assured that He is there. Psalm 34:18 promises, "The LORD is nigh unto them that are of a broken heart." Not only that, but He also knows everything about us, even down to the number of hairs on our head. "Fear not therefore," Jesus says, "ye are of more value than many sparrows" (Luke 12:7). And appearances to the contrary, He truly is working all things, including our grief and sorrow, together for our good and His glory (Romans 8:28).

So, as we walk through this season of grief, let us not lose heart when we look backward and see only one set of footprints behind us. In our darkest moments, our Good Shepherd lovingly sweeps us up into His arms and carries us. We can rest secure in His care.

TODAY'S TAKEAWAY

Even when we can't feel the Lord's presence, we can rest assured that He is with us.

JOURNAL PROMPT

Have there been times during your journey of grief when you have felt abandoned by God? What signs or indications are there that He has in fact been carrying you through this season?

PERSONAL APPLICATION

The following exercises are intended to give you an opportunity to apply the things you're learning and discussing in the group meetings and daily devotionals. They don't have to be done in any particular sequence, or on a particular day of the week. If you only have the physical or emotional energy to complete one of these exercises, that's fine. The point is to allow the Spirit of God to minister to your heart during this time of grief.

CONTRASTING GRIEF AND DESPAIR

Grief is the normal process whereby we mourn a significant loss—for example, a person's death, a divorce, or the loss of a job or career. The key word here is process. It takes time. And, as we saw in Session 1, the process is rarely linear. Grieving persons can move back and forth between different "stages of grief" and can experience them in a different sequence than that in which they are typically presented. All of this is a normal part of the grieving process.

Despair, by contrast, takes things in a different direction. It is typically characterized by a sense of extreme hopelessness or utter meaninglessness. It can leave one feeling desolate and trapped. It goes beyond the normal sadness (even intense sadness) that one normally feels after experiencing a significant loss. Despair paralyzes—and, at its worst, it can fuel thoughts of self-harm or suicidal ideation.

Grief is the heart's way of healing; despair eats away at the heart, destroying hope. Grief is healthy and necessary. Despair is unhealthy and can be dangerous.

- ○ **Action Item:** Look back at the Day Four devotional for this session. Review what you learned there about the characteristics of despair and the lies it tells us. Now, review your journal entries from the other four days of this session and take some time to remind yourself of the truths that God has been revealing to you this week. How do those truths counter the lies spoken by despair? Record your observations here.

ASSESSING YOUR CONDITION—PART THREE

In the last two sessions we looked at our physical and mental condition. In this session and the next, we'll consider how grief is affecting our emotional and spiritual lives. Grief inevitably affects both of these areas, and because they are typically so deeply intertwined, we'll look at them together rather than separately.

Consider the following questions:

- Have you stopped praying because you are angry with God or don't want to spend time with Him?

- Do you find yourself avoiding being around God's people—whether in worship services, fellowship groups, or answering phone calls from members of your church family—because it's too painful emotionally?

- Are you finding yourself so consumed by your grief that you are unable to consider the needs of others, or are you so consumed with taking care of others that you aren't allowing for quiet moments in which God can speak to your heart and meet your emotional and spiritual needs?

If you answered "yes" to any of these questions, know that you're not alone—what you're experiencing is common for many people, including Christians, who are going through grief. The good news is that there is hope: things can turn around for the better.

If you're struggling in one or more of these areas, it doesn't mean that you're failing. But being aware of where you are struggling is helpful in identifying issues to bring to the Lord in prayer and/or ask others to pray about on your behalf.

The goal of this exercise is to encourage you by acknowledging areas where your emotional and spiritual life is strong as well as to help you identify areas where you may not feel quite as strong.

- O **Action Item:** On the next page is a chart listing some characteristics of spiritually-healthy Christians. These are not listed in any particular order, nor is this an exhaustive list. It's simply meant to stimulate your thinking as to what a healthy emotional and spiritual life might look like.

For each of the characteristics listed below, write down some of the ways in which you see that characteristic manifested in your life right now. Be encouraged—the Lord is working in your life, even as you grieve.

Next, consider ways in which that characteristic can be acted on, or practiced,—even when you don't feel strong in it. For each item, one example is given, with additional space provided for you to write down any other ideas you might come up with.

Finally, choose one or two areas in which you are currently weak to take steps of faith by practicing the actions listed in the far right column. You could use the ideas listed in the chart or ones that you come up with on your own.

Spiritually and emotionally healthy Christians . . .	*Some ways in which I see this characteristic in my life are . . .*	*Ways in which this characteristic can be practiced in my life . . .*
Spend time with God (prayer, devotional Bible reading, etc.)		Continue working through this study and do the journaling exercises. *Additional ideas:*
Have confidence in God and that He is at work in their lives.		List several verses about trusting God, and read through them daily. *Additional ideas:*

Spiritually and emotionally healthy Christians . . .	*Some ways in which I see this characteristic in my life are . . .*	*Ways in which this characteristic can be practiced in my life . . .*
Worship God.		Choose a hymn or Christian song that is meaningful to you and sing it to God every day this week. *Additional ideas:*
Recognize that God has a purpose for their lives.		Each day this week, write down one way that God has used or desires to use you in someone else's life. *Additional ideas:*
Spend time alone to think, rest, recover, etc.		Schedule thirty minutes this week to sit by yourself with a notebook to reflect on who God is or how He is working in your life. Do not have a phone or computer nearby. *Additional ideas:*

STABILIZING YOUR SOUL

When our souls are being buffeted by the stormy winds of grief, it's helpful for us to intentionally remind ourselves of God's goodness, providential care, and sovereign reign over every detail of our lives. Unfortunately, it can be difficult to recognize the truth of these realities when we are in the immediate grip of grief. In this session, we looked at three steps of faith that any grief-stricken Christian can take as they follow Christ through the valley of grief.

This exercise is designed to walk you through those steps and give you the opportunity to practice them in your own life. In this session, we'll take a look at the first step, and we'll look at steps 2 and 3 in the next two sessions.

Step of Faith 1: Praise God for who He is.

God's sovereignty and goodness remain, even when we cannot perceive them. As we praise God for His characteristics as revealed in His Word, we exercise faith.

- ○ **Action item:** Look back at your journal entry for the Day 3 devotional in this session, in which you created a written declaration of things you know to be true about God's character that can help you trust His promises. Pick five of the characteristics that you identified and write them down in the space provided here.

Now, spend some time in prayer, praising God for each of these characteristics of His nature.

Over the next five days, take five minutes each day to meditate on one of these characteristics, working your way through the list over the course of those five days.

AND THIS IS THE CONFIDENCE THAT WE HAVE IN HIM, THAT, IF WE ASK ANY THING ACCORDING TO HIS WILL, HE HEARETH US. (1 JOHN 5:14)

5

RELYING ON THE HOLY SPIRIT

WHEN I DON'T KNOW WHAT TO DO

Session Notes

Discussion

Devotional Readings

1. Strength in Weakness
2. When We Don't Know What to Pray
3. The Truth of the Matter
4. A Guide for the Journey
5. How the Holy Spirit Guides

Personal Application

RELYING ON THE HOLY SPIRIT

I JOHN 14

*"Likewise the Spirit also helpeth our infirmities: for we know not what we should pray
for as we ought: but the Spirit itself maketh intercession for us with groanings which
cannot be uttered. 27 And he that searcheth the hearts knoweth what is the mind of
the Spirit, because he maketh intercession for the saints according to the will of God."
(Romans 8:26–27)*

INTRODUCTION

"when I don't know what to do"

1. THE HOLY SPIRIT HELPS WITH OUR problems

"Likewise the Spirit also helpeth our infirmities . . ." (Romans 8:26)

He Abides in Us

*"But now I go my way to him that sent me; and none of you asketh me, Whither
goest thou. 6 But because I have said these things unto you, sorrow hath filled your
heart. 7 Nevertheless I tell you the truth; It is expedient for you that I go away: for
if I go not away, the Comforter will not come unto you; but if I depart, I will send
him unto you." (John 16:5–7)*

"In whom ye also trusted, after that ye heard the word of truth, the gospel of your salvation: in whom also after that ye believed, ye were sealed with that holy Spirit of promise," (Ephesians 1:13)

*"And I will pray the Father, and he shall give you another Comforter, that he may
abide with you for ever; 17 Even the Spirit of truth; whom the world cannot
receive, because it seeth him not, neither knoweth him: but ye know him; for he
dwelleth with you, and shall be in you." (John 14:16–17)*

He Assist Us

"Likewise the Spirit also helpeth our infirmities . . ." (Romans 8:26)

Definition: *Infirmities*—"want of strength, weakness of the body, its native weakness and frailty, feebleness of health or sickness; weakness of the soul, want of strength and capacity requisite to the need."

"Howbeit when he, the Spirit of truth, is come, he will guide you into all truth: for he shall not speak of himself; but whatsoever he shall hear, that shall he speak: and he will shew you things to come." (John 16:13)

"Now we have received, not the spirit of the world, but the spirit which is of God; that we might know the things that are freely given to us of God. 13 Which things also we speak, not in the words which man's wisdom teacheth, but which the Holy Ghost teacheth; comparing spiritual things with spiritual. 14 But the natural man receiveth not the things of the Spirit of God: for they are foolishness unto him: neither can he know them, because they are spiritually discerned." (1 Corinthians 2:12–14)

"And take the helmet of salvation, and the sword of the Spirit, which is the word of God:" (Ephesians 6:17)

"But the Comforter, which is the Holy Ghost, whom the Father will send in my name, he shall teach you all things, and bring all things to your remembrance, I have said unto you." (John 14:26)

"For as many as are led by the Spirit of God, they are the sons of God. 15 For ye have not received the spirit of bondage again to fear; but ye have received the Spirit of adoption, whereby we cry, Abba, Father." (Romans 8:14–15)

2. THE HOLY SPIRIT ASSISTS IN OUR prayers

Quote: *"When thou prayest, rather let thy heart be without words than thy words without heart."*—**John Bunyan**

"Likewise the Spirit also helpeth our infirmities: for we know not what we should pray for as we ought: but the Spirit itself maketh intercession for us with groanings which cannot be uttered. 27 And he that searcheth the hearts knoweth what is the mind of the Spirit, because he maketh intercession for the saints according to the will of God" (Romans 8:26–27)

He instruct Us

Quote: *"God has inspired a psalm for every sigh of the soul. Within the breadth of 150 psalms, you can find the entire range of human emotion. You will never go through anything in life in which you cannot find the root emotions reflected* *in the Psalms. Exhilaration, frustration, discouragement, guilt, forgiveness, joy, gratitude, dealing with enemies, contentment, discontentment—you name it: they are all found in the book of Psalms."*—**Donald Whitney**

"LORD, how are they increased that trouble me! many are they that rise up against me. Many there be which say of my soul, There is no help for him in God. Selah. But thou, O LORD, art a shield for me; my glory, and the lifter up of mine head." (Psalm 3:1–3)

"Fear thou not; for I am with thee: be not dismayed; for I am thy God: I will strengthen thee; yea, I will help thee; yea, I will uphold thee with the right hand of my righteousness." (Isaiah 41:10)

He intercedes for Us

3. THE HOLY SPIRIT DIRECTS OUR purpose

"And he that searcheth the hearts knoweth what is the mind of the Spirit, because he maketh intercession for the saints according to the will of God." (Romans 8:27)

Quote: *"It is strange that, while praying, we seldom ask for change of character, but always a change in circumstance."*—**Unknown**

"And this is the confidence that we have in him, that, if we ask any thing according to his will, he heareth us." (1 John 5:14)

Quote: *"Prayer is surrender—surrender to the will of God and cooperation with that will. If I throw out a boathook from the boat and catch hold of the shore and pull, do I pull the shore to me, or do I pull myself to the shore? Prayer is not pulling God to my will, but the aligning of my will to the will of God."*—**E. Stanley Jones**

THREE COMMANDS RELATED TO THE HOLY SPIRIT

1. ***Be filled with the Spirit***

   "And be not drunk with wine, wherein is excess; but be filled with the Spirit;" (Ephesians 5:18)

2. ***Walk in the Spirit***

   "This I say then, Walk in the Spirit, and ye shall not fulfil the lust of the flesh. . . . 25 If we live in the Spirit, let us also walk in the Spirit." (Galatians 5:16, 25)

3. ***Pray in the Spirit***

   "Praying always with all prayer and supplication in the Spirit, and watching thereunto with all perseverance and supplication for all saints;" (Ephesians 6:18)

CONCLUSION

GROUP DISCUSSION

1. Was there anything from last week's devotionals or application exercises that was particularly meaningful or helpful to you? What passage of Scripture has been most reassuring to you this past week?

2. What does it mean to be filled with the Holy Spirit?

3. What are some scriptural evidences or characteristics of a Christian who is controlled by the Spirit?

4. In this week's session, we mentioned several categories of decisions that can be difficult when one is going through a season of grief, including the following:

- choices specific to the loss we have experienced or are experiencing
- routine decisions of life
- decisions in areas of expertise a loved one used to handle
- decisions for which you cannot seek your loved one's advice
- decisions related directly to the experience of grief

As a group, brainstorm some ways to help one another through the decision-making process. Can you think of resources that may be helpful to someone who is struggling with decisions in one or more of these areas? If so, make a list with relevant details and share it with one another.

5. What is one way the group can pray for you as it relates to grief this week? (A prayer request section is included at the end of this workbook so you can record the requests of other group members.)

SESSION FIVE: DAY ONE

STRENGTH IN WEAKNESS

For we have not an high priest which cannot be touched with the feeling of our infirmities; but was in all points tempted like as we are, yet without sin. (Hebrews 4:15)

Human nature is such that we tend to inflate our virtues and overlook our weaknesses. In reality, however, there is relief in acknowledging the frailty of our lives and our need for God. This is captured well by the Scottish hymn writer Robert Grant in the fourth verse of his hymn "O Worship the King":

> *Frail children of dust, and feeble as frail,*
> *In Thee do we trust, nor find Thee to fail.*
> *Thy mercies, how tender, how firm to the end,*
> *Our Maker, Defender, Redeemer, and Friend!*

In times of grief, we may be tempted to put up a good front, hiding our pain and pretending to have it "all together." The irony, of course, is that this is really unnecessary: most people will be quick to understand that we are going through grief and need. And yet, all too often we're tempted to withdraw behind a façade of false strength.

In one of the great paradoxes of Scripture, the apostle Paul learned that true strength lies in acknowledging our weaknesses and allowing God's strength to shine through them. When he was struggling with his "thorn in the flesh" (2 Corinthians 12:7), Paul asked the Lord three times for healing. In response, the Lord said to him, "My grace is sufficient for thee: for my strength is made perfect in weakness" (2 Corinthians 12:9). In much the same way as light lettering shows up more clearly against a dark background, God's power shows up more obviously against the backdrop of our frailty. And when we see things happening in our lives that can only be explained by God's strength, He receives even more of the glory that He is already due. That is why Paul was able to "glory in [his] infirmities" (2 Corinthians 12:9), not because the infirmities were enjoyable in themselves, but because he recognized that a very good thing—bringing glory to God—was being accomplished through his unpleasant circumstances.

Jesus Himself was, of course, the ultimate picture of "strength in weakness." In taking on human flesh, He limited Himself to a specific time and place and experienced all the frailties that we human beings do—including weariness, fatigue, loneliness, and grief, along with the temptations that come with those experiences. Having experienced human existence in all its weakness and frailty, He knows first-hand what our lives are like.

And because He has experienced human life personally, we can rest assured that He knows the cries of our hearts even when we can't find the words to express them. As Romans 8:26 tells us, "the Spirit itself"—God's Spirit, the Spirit of Christ—"maketh intercession for us with groanings which cannot be uttered."

When we go through a season of grief, what we need is not to be strong or capable or self-sufficient. What we need is to acknowledge our frailties and lean on Christ for His all-sufficient grace.

What we need is God Himself. And that is exactly who we have been given in the presence of the Holy Spirit.

TODAY'S TAKEAWAY

True strength lies in acknowledging our weaknesses and allowing God's power to shine through them.

JOURNAL PROMPT

As you go through your season of grief, are you finding yourself being tempted to put up a false front of strength to those around you? If so, what are some of the specific ways in which you tend to "hide" from others? How might remembering God's strength being made perfect in your weakness help you be able to acknowledge your frailty?

SESSION FIVE: DAY TWO

WHEN WE DON'T KNOW WHAT TO PRAY

Likewise the Spirit also helpeth our infirmities: for we know not what we should pray for as we ought: but the Spirit itself maketh intercession for us with groanings which cannot be uttered. (Romans 8:26)

When we are weighed down by grief, we may not know what to pray for. Bible commentator Alan Barnes observed a number of reasons Christians may not know what to pray for:

1. "They do not know what would be really best for them.
2. They do not know what God might be willing to grant them.
3. They are to a great extent ignorant of the character of God, the reason of His dealings, the principles of His government, and their own real wants.
4. They are often in real, deep perplexity. They are encompassed with trials, exposed to temptations, feeble by disease, and subject to calamities. In these circumstances, if left alone, they would neither be able to bear their trials, nor know what to ask at the hand of God."[1]

All four of these scenarios—and often combinations of them—apply to Christians in times of grief.

The good news is this: in our time of grief, the Holy Spirit instructs us in what we should pray for. One of the ways He does this is by teaching us through His inspired Word.

Think about it: through God's Word, we gain insight into all four areas listed above—what is best for us, what God desires to give us, who God is and how He deals with His people, and His promises that strengthen us for difficulties.

This is why incorporating the words of Scripture into our prayers can be so powerful—we are, in a sense, literally speaking God's "language" back to Him. In so doing, we align our wills with His, effectively echoing the words of the Lord's Prayer: "Thy kingdom come, Thy will be done in earth, as it is in heaven" (Matthew 6:10).

When we don't know what to pray for, Scripture gives us some pointers. We can pray for wisdom: "If any of you lack wisdom, let him ask of God, that giveth to all men liberally, and upbraideth not; and it shall be given him" (James 1:5). The prayer for wisdom is one that our Lord loves to answer. We can choose to give thanks even in the midst of difficult circumstances: "Giving thanks always for all things unto God and the Father in the name of our Lord Jesus Christ" (Ephesians 5:20). And we can pray that God's name would be honored in our lives and in the world around us: "After this manner therefore pray ye: Our Father which art in heaven, Hallowed be thy name" (Matthew 6:9). And that's just for starters; Scripture provides us with a whole host of prayer prompts covering a wide range of concerns and circumstances.

God wants to hear from us, even when we are in the depths of grief. Thankfully, He has given us His words to speak when we can't come up with words of our own. And we have the assurance that as we come to God in prayer, the Spirit takes the words we speak—even our wordless groans—and uses them as a basis for interceding with the Father on our behalf.

TODAY'S TAKEAWAY

When we don't know how to pray or what to pray for, the Holy Spirit instructs us in what to pray—using especially the words of Scripture itself—and expresses the deepest groanings of our hearts as He intercedes on our behalf before the Father.

JOURNAL PROMPT

Take a passage of Scripture that has been particularly meaningful to you recently and use it as the basis for a prayer. Write out the verse(s) and the prayer in the space provided here.

SESSION FIVE: DAY THREE

THE TRUTH OF THE MATTER

Howbeit when he, the Spirit of truth, is come, he will guide you into all truth . . . (John 16:13)

Mammoth Cave in Kentucky is the longest known cave system on Earth, with some four hundred miles of underground tunnels, caverns, and rivers mapped to date. Each year more than two million people from around the world visit. Not far inside the cave is a large opening known as "The Cathedral." In the 1800s, churches sometimes held services there, with the preacher standing on what became known as "Pulpit Rock" to address the congregation. It is said that on one tour, the guide stopped his group in that spot and told them he was going to preach to them. Climbing up on the rock he said, "Stay close to your guide!"

That is a sermon that every Christian—especially one who is navigating the journey of grief—needs to hear again and again.

Before Jesus left Earth to return to Heaven, he promised His disciples that He would send "another Comforter, that he may abide with you for ever; Even the Spirit of truth" (John 14:16–17). The Holy Spirit, Jesus promised, "will guide you into all truth" (John 16:13).

How does the Spirit guide us into all truth? One of the principal ways He does this is by revealing to us and helping us to understand Jesus, who is Himself the very embodiment of truth. As Jesus put it in John 14:6, "I am the way, the truth, and the life." The closer we get to and the more deeply we know Jesus, the more we will know and understand the truth about God and who we are in relationship to Him.

Often, the Holy Spirit uses His people to speak His truth into our hearts. And sometimes He even uses the beauty of nature to remind us that He is with us. In those times when we need it most, the Spirit "itself beareth witness with our spirit, that we are the children of God" (Romans 8:16).

"Ye shall know the truth, and the truth shall make you free," Jesus told his followers in John 8:32. When we say we know that "Jesus is Lord," we're not just expressing a hunch, hope, or wish. No, we're expressing a *certainty* that Jesus reigns supreme, that He is providentially working to accomplish His purposes, and that one day all things will be subject to Him (Ephesians 1:10) as He establishes a never-ending kingdom of justice and peace in which every tear is wiped away (Revelation 21:4). These are truths that the Spirit of God reveals and confirms to us. And, as we nourish our souls with these truths, we can find a freedom and sense of joy that even the deepest sorrow cannot extinguish.

TODAY'S TAKEAWAY

The Holy Spirit guides us into knowledge of the truths about who God is and who we are in relationship to Him. As we nourish our souls with these truths, we can find a freedom and sense of joy that even the deepest sorrow cannot extinguish.

JOURNAL PROMPT

What is one truth that the Spirit of God has revealed to you during this season of grief about who He is and who you are in relationship to Him?

SESSION FIVE: DAY FOUR

A GUIDE FOR THE JOURNEY

I will instruct thee and teach thee in the way which thou shalt go: I will guide thee with mine eye. (Psalm 32:8)

Kelly Gallagher won a gold medal at the Paralympic Winter Games in 2014 in slalom skiing. Slalom skiing reaches speeds of 60 mph, which is difficult enough, but what is most amazing is that Gallagher has a medical condition which makes her almost completely blind. She navigates the course by listening to her guide over a Bluetooth headset. Her guide skis the course just in front of her and gives her instructions all the way down.

The Holy Spirit often guides us in much the same way—step by step, turn by turn, choice by choice, moment by moment. Frequently, He shows us only a little bit of the path ahead of us at any given time. But just as Kelly has a reliable guide leading her down the mountain, so we can trust that we have a trustworthy guide for our journey through grief and beyond.

Part of the journey of faith, especially during times of grief, is learning to "walk in the Spirit" (Galatians 5:16, 25) on a daily basis. This is not always easy, but it is something in which we can grow and mature. Ultimately, being under the control of the Holy Spirit boils down to the daily, moment-by-moment choices we make. It's a repeated decision to say "no" to our fleshly impulses and say "yes" to the Holy Spirit's direction.

Because of the blood of Jesus shed on the cross, and through the power of the Holy Spirit that indwells us, we are now able to "come boldly unto the throne of grace, that we may obtain mercy, and find grace to help in time of need" (Hebrews 4:16). When we enter the throne room of our Heavenly Father, we are able to find grace not only for salvation itself, but also for living day by day—especially through times of grief and sorrow.

The reality of God's readily-available grace is especially important in times of grief, when our ability to see the path ahead of us is often severely impaired. In such times, we need the guidance of the Holy Spirit more than ever. Fortunately, the Lord promises to guide us: "I will instruct thee and teach thee in the way which thou shalt go: I will guide thee with mine eye" (Psalm 32:8). This is good news: we don't have to try to figure out our way; we can rely on the Lord to lead us, by His Spirit, along the path He has set out for us.

When we yield to the Holy Spirit's direction, we will find we have the best guide we could ever have for the journey. That doesn't mean the journey itself will be easy or without difficulty, but it does mean that we can rest assured that we have a guide who will never lead us astray. And in our time of grief, that may be the most important thing we need to know.

TODAY'S TAKEAWAY

You can trust the Holy Spirit as your guide. He will never lead you astray, but will always lead you to truth.

JOURNAL PROMPT

What is a Scripture passage that God has recently been using in your life to give you guidance?

SESSION FIVE: DAY FIVE

HOW THE HOLY SPIRIT GUIDES

Howbeit when he, the Spirit of truth, is come, he will guide you into all truth: for he shall not speak of himself; but whatsoever he shall hear, that shall he speak: and he will shew you things to come. (John 16:13)

One summer, when our children were teens, during a family vacation we went rafting on the Shoshone River in Wyoming. Before allowing us to rent the rafts and hire a guide, the company basically required us to sign our lives away: "I understand the risks involved and will not hold my guide responsible for dismemberment, loss of life, or…." I signed on the dotted line.

Once we reached the river, the guide continued the warnings. He explained that he would only be able to help us if we recognized that he was in charge and committed to follow his directions on our journey. Once on the raft, I quickly understood the warnings and the necessity of having a guide. We could never have navigated those raging rapids by ourselves.

Sometimes during the journey, I silently questioned the wisdom of the guide as he would direct us to areas that seemed dangerous to me. It looked to us like we would capsize the raft by steering where he directed, but he knew the safest spots, and I'm thankful we followed his instructions.

One of the divine ministries of the Holy Spirit is to guide us. John 16:13 promises, "Howbeit when he, the Spirit of truth, is come, he will guide you into all truth: for he shall not speak of himself; but whatsoever he shall hear, that shall he speak: and he will shew you things to come."

Throughout our entire Christian journey, it is essential that we submit to the guidance of the Holy Spirit. And this is never more needful than during seasons of grief. To navigate this season and come out the other side all in one piece, we need to yield to His control and follow His leading.

Consider these three ways the Holy Spirit guides us:

In accordance with Scripture: Truth is the foundation for all the Holy Spirit does in the believer's life. Notice how in John 16:13 Christ referred to the Holy Spirit as "the Spirit of truth." He will never guide us away from the truth but always to the truth and with the truth.

Scripture is God's revealed truth, and the Holy Spirit uses it powerfully in our lives. Ephesians 6:17 commands "And take...the sword of the Spirit, which is the word of God." Allowing the Holy Spirit to use God's Word in our lives is vital to spiritual victory.

With compliance to the Savior: There is perfect unity within the trinity. The Holy Spirit always guides us by what He hears from the Son, and He speaks in harmony with the Father's will for our lives. John 16:13 says, "Howbeit when he, the Spirit of truth, is come, he will guide you into all truth: for he shall not speak of himself; but whatsoever he shall hear, that shall he speak: and he will shew you things to come."

To actions of obedience: Knowing God's instructions for our lives is not enough; we must do what we know we should do (James 1:22). As I wake up each morning, I purposefully surrender to the Holy Spirit. I tell Him that I give Him complete control of my day and that I yield myself to Him. Then throughout the day, I strive to obey every impulse of the Spirit.

TODAY'S TAKEAWAY

We don't have to navigate each day with our own wisdom and in the power of the flesh. We have a divine Guide—one who has already charted our course and has committed Himself to steering us through the rapids of life—and the dangers of grief.

JOURNAL PROMPT

How has the Holy Spirit been providing direction through this journey of grief? What from this week's session or devotions has been part of His direction in your life?

PERSONAL APPLICATION

The following exercises are intended to give you an opportunity to apply the things you're learning and discussing in the group meetings and daily devotionals. They don't have to be done in any particular sequence or on a particular day of the week. If you only have the physical or emotional energy to complete one of these exercises, that's fine. The point is to allow the Spirit of God to minister to your heart during this time of grief.

MAKING DECISIONS WHEN YOU DON'T KNOW WHAT TO DO

In times of decision, one of the most helpful questions we can ask is, "What does the Bible say about this area of life?" By looking to Scripture and to people who know God's Word, we'll be better able to separate the more consequential decisions from less consequential decisions. And in all areas, we'll be reminded of the Holy Spirit's presence as He points us to Christ and reaffirms to us the tender love of our Heavenly Father.

O **Action Item:** Think about the pressing decisions you may be facing at the moment. For each decision, fill in any applicable responses to the following:

Decision #1

- The issue at stake is:

____

____

- The specific options available are:

____

____

- The relevant considerations with regard to this decision are:

____

____

- What does the Bible have to say about this area of life?

____

____

- What input (if any) have I received from godly Christian advisors regarding this issue?

- To the best of my ability to discern, what is the Holy Spirit saying to me about this issue?

- For now, my decision with regard to this issue is:

Repeat as needed.

ASSESSING YOUR CONDITION – PART FOUR

In the last three sessions we looked at our physical and mental condition, and also began looking at our emotional and spiritual lives. In this session, we finish up our consideration of how our emotional and spiritual lives are being affected by our grief.

○ **Action item:** Following is a chart listing some additional characteristics of spiritually healthy Christians. As with last week, they are not listed in any particular order of priority, nor is this an exhaustive list. It's simply meant to stimulate your thinking as to what a healthy emotional and spiritual life might look like.

For each of the characteristics listed, write down some of the ways in which you see that characteristic manifested in your life right now. *Be encouraged*—the Lord is working in your life, even as you grieve.

Next, consider ways in which that characteristic can be acted on, or practiced,—even when you don't feel strong in it. For each item, one example is given, with additional space provided for you to write down any other ideas you might come up with.

Finally, choose one or two areas in which you are currently weak to take steps of faith by practicing the actions listed in the far right column. You could use the ideas listed in the chart or ones that you come up with on your own.

Spiritually and emotionally healthy Christians . . .	*Some ways in which I see this characteristic in my life are . . .*	*Ways in which this characteristic can be practiced in my life . . .*
Take care of themselves.		Identify one area of needed focus for your health (sleep, alone time, healthy eating, etc.), and plan one actionable step you can take in that area this week. *Additional ideas:*
Stay connected to God's people.		Instead of watching church online, go to a live service—even if you need to sit in the back. *Additional ideas:*
Serve and care for others.		Take a grocery gift card to a local food ministry. *Additional ideas:*

Spiritually and emotionally healthy Christians . . .	*Some ways in which I see this characteristic in my life are . . .*	*Ways in which this characteristic can be practiced in my life . . .*
Desire to share the gospel with others.		Hand a gospel tract out to at least one person this week. *Additional ideas:*
Are grateful.		Write and send a thank-you card to someone you appreciate. *Additional ideas:*

STABILIZING YOUR SOUL

When our souls are buffeted by the stormy winds of grief, it's helpful to intentionally remind ourselves of God's goodness, providential care, and sovereign reign over every detail of our lives. In Session 4, we learned about three steps of faith we can take to follow Christ through the valley of grief. This exercise is designed to help you take those steps. In our last session, we looked at one step. In this session, we'll look at a second step, and then we'll finish with a third in the next session.

Step of Faith 2: Pour out your heart to God, including your pain, and express your trust in Him.

Sometimes we think that expressing pain to God reveals a lack of faith. The truth is that not expressing the pain we feel to God is a lack of faith. Pouring out your heart to God in confidence that He hears and cares and then choosing to trust in Him—that's faith.

O **Action item:** Read Psalm 13 and Psalm 77. Using these psalms as a model, write out your own faith-filled lament to God. Here are some guiding questions to help you get started:

a. What are the "complaints" you'd like to bring before God? For example,

- Things in your life that feel out of control
- Specific problems, struggles, or difficulties
- Unanswered questions

b. How can what you know to be true about God's character, and the memories of things He has done for you in the past, help you now to make the choice to trust Him in these areas?

c. How can you express your decision to trust God—in words, actions, or attitudes—in spite of the circumstances and challenges you're facing?

Space is provided here to record your lament to God. As you write, don't worry about style or format—the point isn't to try to replicate one of the psalms. The point, rather, is simply to provide an opportunity for you to pour your heart out honestly before God—and in doing so, to exercise your faith in this moment of grief.

AND WE KNOW THAT ALL THINGS WORK TOGETHER FOR GOOD TO THEM THAT LOVE GOD, TO THEM WHO ARE THE CALLED ACCORDING TO HIS PURPOSE. (ROMANS 8:28)

CLAIMING GOD'S PROMISE

WHEN I DON'T UNDERSTAND

Session Notes

Discussion

Devotional Readings

1. Working All Things for Good
2. When Our Steps Are Redirected
3. God Meant It for Good
4. Grief and Forgiveness
5. Knowing the Truth of God's Promises

Personal Application

CLAIMING GOD'S PROMISE

"And we know that all things work together for good to them that love God, to them who are the called according to his purpose. 29 For whom he did foreknow, he also did predestinate to be conformed to the image of his Son, that he might be the firstborn among many brethren." (Romans 8:28–29)

INTRODUCTION

when I don't understand

____

____

Quote: *"Romans 8:28 is a soft pillow for a tired heart."*—**R. A. Torrey**

1. THE Promise

And We Know

"For I know that my redeemer liveth, and that he shall stand at the latter day upon the earth:" (Job 19:25)

"These things have I written unto you that believe on the name of the Son of God; that ye may know that ye have eternal life, and that ye may believe on the name of the Son of God." (1 John 5:13)

"For the which cause I also suffer these things: nevertheless I am not ashamed: for I know whom I have believed, and am persuaded that he is able to keep that which I have committed unto him against that day." (2 Timothy 1:12)

Quote: *"God never made a promise that was too good to be true. They are all good and they are all true."*—**D. L. Moody**

That All Things

"Who shall separate us from the love of Christ? shall tribulation, or distress, or persecution, or famine, or nakedness, or peril, or sword?... 37 Nay, in all these things we are more than conquerors through him that loved us." (Romans 8:35, 37)

Quote: *God can make all, and does make all, work ultimately for our good. . . . Trials and tribulations and failures and sin are not good in and of themselves, and it is folly to pretend that they are. They are bad. How then can we justify the statement that all of them "work together for good"? The answer is that they are so used by God, and so over-ruled by God and employed by God that they turn out for our good."*
—Martyn Lloyd-Jones

Work together

*"And Mordecai went out from the presence of the king in royal apparel of blue and
white, and with a great crown of gold, and with a garment of fine linen and purple:
and the city of Shushan rejoiced and was glad. 16 The Jews had light, and gladness,
and joy, and honour. 17 And in every province, and in every city, whithersoever
the king's commandment and his decree came, the Jews had joy and gladness, a
feast and a good day. And many of the people of the land became Jews; for the fear
of the Jews fell upon them." (Esther 8:15–17)*

"But as for you, ye thought evil against me; but God meant it unto good, to bring to pass, as it is this day, to save much people alive." (Genesis 50:20)

*"But I would ye should understand, brethren, that the things which happened unto
me have fallen out rather unto the furtherance of the gospel; 13 So that my bonds
in Christ are manifest in all the palace, and in all other places; 14 And many of the
brethren in the Lord, waxing confident by my bonds, are much more bold to speak
the word without fear" (Philippians 1:12–14)*

Quote: *"There is no attribute of God more comforting to His children than that of divine sovereignty. Under the most adverse circumstances, in the most severe trials, they believe that sovereignty has ordained their afflictions, that sovereignty overrules them, and that sovereignty will sanctify them all."*—**Charles Spurgeon**

For good

"He that spared not his own Son, but delivered him up for us all, how shall he not with him also freely give us all things?" (Romans 8:32)

Quote: *"Romans 8:28 is a flower of grace growing on the slopes of Calvary."*
—Robert Morgan

God works all things together for the good for them that loves God

"And were beyond measure astonished, saying, He hath done all things well: he maketh both the deaf to hear, and the dumb to speak." (Mark 7:37)

Quote: *"To the child of God, there is no such thing as an accident. . . . Accidents may indeed appear to befall him and misfortune stalk his way; but these evils will be so in appearance only and will seem evils only because we cannot read the secret script of God's hidden providence."*—**A. W. Tozer**

2. THE people

"And we know that all things work together for good to them that love God, to them who are the called according to his purpose." (Romans 8:28)

To Them That love God

"We love him, because he first loved us." (1 John 4:19)

"For I am persuaded, that neither death, nor life, nor angels, nor principalities, nor powers, nor things present, nor things to come, 39 Nor height, nor depth, nor any other creature, shall be able to separate us from the love of God, which is in Christ Jesus our Lord." (Romans 8:38–39)

To Them Who Are the called

"Unto the church of God which is at Corinth, to them that are sanctified in Christ Jesus, called to be saints, with all that in every place call upon the name of Jesus Christ our Lord, both theirs and ours: . . . 9 God is faithful, by whom ye were called unto the fellowship of his Son Jesus Christ our Lord." (1 Corinthians 1:2, 9)

According to His purpose

"For we are his workmanship, created in Christ Jesus unto good works, which God hath before ordained that we should walk in them." (Ephesians 2:10)

"Behold, I go forward, but he is not there; and backward, but I cannot perceive him: 9 On the left hand, where he doth work, but I cannot behold him: he hideth himself on the right hand, that I cannot see him: 10 But he knoweth the way that I take: when he hath tried me, I shall come forth as gold." (Job 23:8–10)

"When my spirit was overwhelmed within me, then thou knewest my path. In the way wherein I walked have they privily laid a snare for me. 4 I looked on my right hand, and beheld, but there was no man that would know me: refuge failed me;

no man cared for my soul. 5 I cried unto thee, O LORD: I said, Thou art my refuge and my portion in the land of the living." (Psalm 142:3–5)

Quote: *"God is too good to be unkind and He is too wise to be mistaken. And when we cannot trace His hand, we must trust His heart."*—**Charles Spurgeon**

3. THE Process

"And we know that all things work together for good to them that love God, to them who are the called according to his purpose. 29 For whom he did foreknow, he also did predestinate to be conformed to the image of his Son, that he might be the firstborn among many brethren." (Romans 8:28–29)

Definition: *Foreknow*, from Greek *proginōskō*—to have knowledge of beforehand

Definition: *Predestinate,* from Greek *proorizō*—to foreordain, to determine beforehand

"The steps of a good man are ordered by the LORD: and he delighteth in his way." (Psalm 37:23)

"Moreover whom he did predestinate, them he also called: and whom he called, them he also justified: and whom he justified, them he also glorified." (Romans 8:30)

Quote: *"A sick bed often teaches more than a sermon."*—**Thomas Watson**

CONCLUSION

GROUP DISCUSSION

1. Was there anything from last week's devotionals or application exercises that was particularly meaningful or helpful to you? What passage of Scripture has been most reassuring to you this past week?

2. When you are grieving, clichés can feel hurtful. What makes God's promises, including Romans 8:28, different than a cliché?

3. What are some ways in which you've seen God work "all things . . . together for good" in your life in the past? How does this give you hope for your present and future?

4. When grief threatens to swallow you up, what are some practical ways in which you can hold on to God's promises (especially Romans 8:28)?

5. What is one way the group can pray for you as it relates to grief this week? (A prayer request section is included at the end of this workbook so you can record the requests of other group members.)

SESSION SIX: DAY ONE

WORKING ALL THINGS FOR GOOD

And we know that all things work together for good to them that love God, to them who are the called according to his purpose. (Romans 8:28)

God's providence is always at work—both on global and personal levels. Sometimes, however, in the warp and woof of everyday life, we can't see what God is doing in our own lives or in the lives of those we love. This can be especially true during seasons of grief. In such times, it can be helpful to take a step back to consider how God has acted in the grand sweep of history to accomplish His purposes. In this regard, the pages of Scripture are instructive.

Consider, for example, the biblical story of the tower of Babel (Genesis 11). Instead of fulfilling the creation mandate to "be fruitful, and multiply, and replenish the earth" (Genesis 1:28)—a command that was reiterated to Noah and his descendants after the flood (Genesis 9:7)—people had begun to congregate in one place. Even worse, they allowed their sinful pride to get in the way of obedience to God's command. They decided to build a city with a tower that would reach to the very heavens: "let us make us a name," they said, "lest we be scattered abroad upon the face of the whole earth" (Genesis 11:4).

In response to this rebellion, God imposed judgment on the people by confusing their languages. People who had been able to communicate without any difficulty the previous day could no longer understand each other. They now had no choice but to fan out in separate directions, forming distinct peoples, nations, and cultures—precisely what God had commanded in the first place.

Note that what originally began in sinful pride and rebellion was turned around by God to accomplish His purposes. In fact, God even used this event as one part of His larger plan of redemption. How so?

Through the fulfillment of the creation mandate to populate the earth, distinct people groups and nations were formed, helping to set the stage for the eventual arrival of the Messiah through Israel, God's special "peculiar" people (1 Peter 2:9). And, to this day, we enjoy the diversity of human languages (some 7,000–8,000 at present count), cultures, foods, and customs that came about as a result of this spreading of humanity throughout the earth. Indeed, one of the great promises of Scripture is that God will one day gather people from "all nations, and kindreds, and people, and tongues" (Revelation 7:9) into fellowship with Him and one another for all eternity. Talk about working all things for good!

The pages of Scripture are replete with examples of God's providential activity in the lives of His people, at both the individual level and that of larger groups, including the nation of Israel. He uses the righteous acts of His followers and the evil acts of those who oppose Him—all for His glory and for the good of His people. He carefully weaves all things—even those that, by themselves, are bad or evil—into a tapestry that furthers His eternally good purposes for His creation. For those who bear the weight of grief resulting from their own sin or from having been sinned against, this is good news: our Redeemer *will* redeem. For all of us, this can provide genuine hope even as we grieve.

TODAY'S TAKEAWAY

Reflecting on the ways in which God has worked providentially throughout history can help us trust in His providential work in our own lives today—even in our time of grief and sorrow.

JOURNAL PROMPT

How does reflecting on God's providential activity in the past encourage you in your current time of grief?

SESSION SIX: DAY TWO

WHEN OUR STEPS ARE REDIRECTED

Trust in the LORD with all thine heart; and lean not unto thine own understanding. In all thy ways acknowledge him, and he shall direct thy paths. (Proverbs 3:5–6)

When George Washington was eleven years old, his father, who was only forty-nine, passed away. This loss would prove to create a monumental turn of events, forever altering the trajectory of Washington's life. As one biographer of Washington explains, well-to-do young men of George Washington's day were typically shipped off from the American colonies to England to receive a classical college education, thereby securing an expected future of wealth, prestige, and career success. But when George's father died, his prospects were significantly narrowed. Going to college in England became a practical impossibility, so he had to find other avenues for professional and personal success. As it turned out, he ended up finding work as a surveyor of the vast, unmapped territories in and around the colony of Virginia. This accustomed him to spending extended time in the unforgiving terrain through which he would later lead troops during the Revolutionary War. In this way, he gained experience that would prove vital to sustaining the Continental army's morale as they faced a long, harsh winter of near-starvation and deprivation at Valley Forge, Pennsylvania.[1]

We never know how our current circumstances may be preparing us for future service to others and, ultimately, to the Kingdom of Heaven.

Another couple who experienced God's redirection of their steps was Bill and Cathy Rice, whose lives changed dramatically after their baby daughter Betty contracted spinal meningitis and, as a result, lost her hearing. Bill and Cathy initially grieved the loss of the dreams they had held for their daughter, but over time, as they traveled the country with Bill preaching as an evangelist, the Rices found themselves with a burden to reach out to people with hearing impairments, so that they too might be able to receive and respond to the gospel. The result was the founding of the Bill Rice Ranch in 1953, through which thousands of people—deaf and hearing alike—have since come to Christ.

When grief enters our lives, our well-laid plans can be shattered. Circumstances may dictate drastic changes in our lives. In such times, we must remember that although our *steps* may change, our *purpose* never changes. We are servants of God, called and enabled to share His love and the truth of His gospel wherever we go.

So, how should we respond when life throws the proverbial "curve ball" our way? Perhaps the most important thing we can do is follow the admonition of Proverbs 3:5–6: "Trust in the Lord with all thine heart; and lean not unto thine own understanding. In all thy ways acknowledge him, and he shall direct thy paths." When we put our trust in the Lord and His infinite wisdom, we have a promise we can count on: He will direct our paths.

TODAY'S TAKEAWAY

When our steps are redirected by grief and disappointments, we can rest assured that our lives still have meaning and purpose and that God will guide us well on the new path He has set before us.

JOURNAL PROMPT

In God's hands, the disappointments of our lives are often gateways into new, unimagined opportunities for growth and kingdom service. Do you sense any new opportunities that the Lord may be opening up for you, even as you go through this season of grief?

SESSION SIX: DAY THREE

GOD MEANT IT FOR GOOD

And Joseph said unto them, Fear not: for am I in the place of God? But as for you, ye thought evil against me; but God meant it unto good, to bring to pass, as it is this day, to save much people alive. Now therefore fear ye not: I will nourish you, and your little ones. And he comforted them, and spake kindly unto them. (Genesis 50:19–21)

Samuel Logan Brengle was a worker with the Salvation Army in Boston many years ago. As he passed by a saloon, some men threw a brick at his head. Their aim was good, and Brengle nearly died. As it was, he spent eighteen months in recovery. During that time he wrote a little book entitled *Helps to Holiness*. Thousands of copies were published. After he was able to begin preaching again, people would often thank him for the book. He would respond by saying, "If there had been no little brick, there had been no little book." His wife saved the brick and had Genesis 50:20 engraved on it.

The difference between people who trust God even through difficult times and trials and those who do not is found in the way they view those trials. Godly Christians have the same problems, heartbreaks, and tragedies as everyone else. They are not somehow exempt from suffering. But they view their difficult circumstances through the lens of an understanding of God's love and purpose for their lives.

One preacher said it well, "The only thing an enemy can do to you is to be the unwitting instrument of God's plan for your life." Of course many things happen that are painful and hard for us to endure. Yet those circumstances do not mean God has forgotten or forsaken us. He makes "all things work together for good" (Romans 8:28). This helps us understand that even the most difficult things we experience are a necessary part of His plan.

Joseph's story in the Old Testament is an example of this truth. His brothers absolutely meant to harm him when they sold him into slavery. But what they intended for harm, God repurposed for good. Joseph's confidence in God's power and providence in his life is seen in his statement of forgiveness to his brothers in the verses above. His statement almost sounds like an Old Testament version of Romans 8:28.

God's providence is not just reactive, but it is strategically anticipative in our lives. Even when our griefs are caused by the evil intentions of others, God can bring healing to our hearts and make all things work together for good.

TODAY'S TAKEAWAY

God has not forgotten nor forsaken you, and He never will. He is always at work in His children's lives to make all things work together for good.

JOURNAL PROMPT

Examples of the truth of Romans 8:28 are all throughout the Bible. What one or two stories in addition to Joseph's can you think of in which God made the evil plans of others work together for the good of His child?

SESSION SIX: DAY FOUR

GRIEF AND FORGIVENESS

Then said Jesus, Father, forgive them; for they know not what they do. . . . (Luke 23:34)

One of the most memorable images from the Vietnam War is a famous picture that shows a nine year old girl running down a road, her arms outstretched and terror etched on her face. Her village, Trảng Bàng, had just been struck with a napalm bomb by the South Vietnamese air force, and the little girl—Phan Thị Kim Phúc, popularly known as "the girl in the picture" or "the napalm girl"—was severely burned on her back and shoulders when her clothing caught fire in the bombing. "It's burning! It's burning!" she was screaming as she ran down the road toward a group of journalists who were covering the conflict.

After taking the Pulitzer Prize-winning picture, photographer Nick Ut helped get Kim Phúc to a hospital in Saigon, where she was hospitalized for fourteen months and underwent seventeen surgeries. She eventually returned home to her family, but her recovery was far from over. She later had to undergo additional surgeries and procedures to further restore function and mobility, and she has lived with severe pain and significant physical limitations since the day of the bombing. In the decades that have passed, Kim has become a Canadian citizen, has married, and has two children.

But the story of Kim's recovery does not end there. It was one thing to heal her physical wounds; it was another thing altogether to heal the emotional and spiritual scars that developed after the events of that day. The pain and grief she experienced over the subsequent years fueled an intense hatred toward those who had caused this suffering in her life.

By God's grace, Kim eventually found a copy of the Bible in a library in Vietnam. Through reading the Bible and then responding to a friend's invitation to attend church, Kim heard the gospel and eventually trusted Christ as her Savior. Over time, as the Lord worked healing in her heart, she was able to publicly forgive those whom she had previously viewed as her enemies, and she went on to establish a foundation that works to provide medical and psychological support to children who are suffering as a result of war. Kim's story is an illustration of how God can take the tragedies of our lives and use them to work His good purposes.

Grief and the need for forgiveness can go hand in hand. Great grief can come into our lives because of other people's sin against us. But if we hold onto bitterness and anger, we will not heal in our grief.

When we struggle to forgive, it's helpful to remember that God's promise in Romans 8:28 is an ironclad guarantee that God will take *all* the circumstances of our lives—even the most painful and grievous—and work them together to accomplish His good purposes for us. As we rely in faith upon that great promise, we can be empowered to follow in the footsteps of our Lord and Savior in saying, *"Father, forgive* . . . ."

TODAY'S TAKEAWAY

Relying upon the promise of Romans 8:28—that God will work even the most difficult circumstances of our lives to accomplish His good purposes for us—can give us the strength to choose to forgive.

JOURNAL PROMPT

Are there people you are struggling to forgive? If so, ask the Lord to help you choose forgiveness in light of the promise of Romans 8:28.

SESSION SIX: DAY FIVE

KNOWING THE TRUTH OF GOD'S PROMISES

. . . that ye, . . . May be able to comprehend with all saints what is the breadth, and length, and depth, and height; And to know the love of Christ, which passeth knowledge, that ye might be filled with all the fulness of God. (Ephesians 3:17–19)

We saw in this week's group study that God wants us to *know* the truth of His promises, including that of Romans 8:28.

There are many things that have always been true about our world, although people did not always know. Consider, for example, some of the major scientific discoveries that have revolutionized our world:

- The fact that the earth is round rather than flat.
- The nature of electricity.
- The structure of the atom.
- The nature of gravity.

Each of these realties was always true, but we humans didn't always *know* them—they had to be discovered. Once discovered, though, that newfound knowledge enabled us to do all sorts of things we had previously been unable to do:

- Understanding that the earth is round rather than flat made it possible to circumnavigate the globe via water.
- Understanding the nature of electricity made it possible for us to light our homes more efficiently and helped fuel the industrial revolution.
- Understanding the structure of the atom opened up new sources of energy and facilitated the development of vastly more powerful weapons.
- Understanding the nature of gravity helped us learn how to send astronauts into space and land them on the moon.

Thankfully, God reveals to us in His Word the things that He wants us to know about Him, ourselves, and our relationship with Him. One of the things He wants us to know is how high, deep, and wide the love of Christ is for us. In his letter to the Ephesians, Paul prays that his readers would "be able to comprehend with all saints what is the breadth, and length, and depth, and height; And to know the love of Christ, which passeth knowledge, that ye might be filled with all the fulness of God" (Ephesians 3:18–19). God's promises to us are rooted in His boundless love for us, and because "love never fails" (1 Corinthians 13:8)—especially *God's* love—we can rest assured that His promises, too, will never fail us.

"Ye shall know the truth, and the truth shall make you free," Jesus said to those who challenged his identity and authority (John 8:32). Biblically speaking, knowledge of the truth is not merely intellectual; it is relational. It involves an intimate reception of the very person of Christ Himself, who gave His life *for* us and promises, in turn, to give His life *to* us.

Knowing and trusting in the truths of God's promises frees us, even as we grieve. It frees us for *thanksgiving*—we can sincerely thank God for His goodness to us even as we undergo the pain of loss. It frees us for *lament*—we can grieve honestly before our Heavenly Father, knowing that we are forever secure in His undying love. And it frees us for *hope*—knowing that God will set right all that is wrong with this world, we can endure the trials of today in light of the future that awaits us.

TODAY'S TAKEAWAY

God's promises are rooted in his limitless love for us, and therefore will never fail. Thus, knowing the truth of His promises frees us for thanksgiving, lament, and hope even as we grieve.

JOURNAL PROMPT

What is one thing for which you are thankful today? What is one thing that you are sorrowful about? And what is one thing that gives you hope?

PERSONAL APPLICATION

The following exercises are intended to give you an opportunity to apply the things you're learning and discussing in the group meetings and daily devotionals. They don't have to be done in any particular sequence or on a particular day of the week. If you only have the physical or emotional energy to complete one of these exercises, that's fine. The point is to allow the Spirit of God to minister to your heart during this time of grief.

DECLARING GOD'S PROMISES

Kim Phúc (who we met in Day 4), shared that when that famous picture was taken she was screaming, "It's burning, it's burning." In the midst of trials, it can seem like all that we know and care about is burning down around us. The discouragement of grief in particular can tell us that life is a continuous trail of meaningless and out-of-control events, a fatalistic train ride that is doomed to destruction.

When we're struggling with these feelings, acknowledging them and then declaring the truth of God's Word into our lives can build our trust in His promises.

- [ ] **Action Item:** Find a quiet place this week where you can pray aloud (even loudly, if needed) to God about the situations, people, fears, or losses that are burning anxiety or sorrow into your soul. When you are done, pray a declaration of truth, based on the promises of God in Scripture that you read this week.

  Example: "My body hurts and this disease may end my life."
  Declaration based on Proverbs 3:5–6: "I will trust in you, Lord, even though I don't understand. You are my Savior, and I will follow you no matter what."

PRACTICING YOUR PURPOSE

And God is able to make all grace abound toward you; that ye, always having all sufficiency in all things, may abound to every good work. (2 Corinthians 9:8)

Salvation is the not the end, but the beginning of all that God has called us to. And although it may feel at times that grief has overwhelmed every other purpose of our lives, we can be assured in knowing that God's great calling for us is larger than the loss we have experienced.

Grief has a way of robbing us of the activities and interests that used to excite us. In time, these interests may return. But don't feel the need to force them. Instead, lean into the purpose for which you were created—knowing God and making Him known.

Even as you grieve, you can still hold on to and fulfill God's purposes for you. It can be as simple as a "not-so-random" act of kindness.

- ○ **Action item:** Choose one person who does not yet know Jesus as their Savior to receive a "not-so-random act of kindness" from you. It can be as simple as clipping some flowers out of your yard and taking them to the receptionist at your gym. Whatever you do, make it simple and easy and something that will express love to someone else. And know that in doing so, you're continuing to fulfill your purpose—sharing the love of God wherever you go.

STABILIZING YOUR SOUL

There are three steps of faith that any grief-stricken Christian can take as they follow Christ through the valley of grief. This exercise is designed to walk you through those steps and give you the opportunity to practice them in your own life.

In Sessions 4 and 5, we looked at the first two steps. In this session, we'll complete our three-part series by looking at step 3.

Step of Faith 3: Persist in fulfilling regular responsibilities and worship.

Sometimes, when you're not sure of the next step and you're waiting for the Lord's guidance, the best thing you can do is take a step of faith by remaining faithful to the commitments you already have in front of you.

Take a few moments to think about your current responsibilities and how they might factor into a life of faithfulness as you wait upon the Lord for His leading and guidance.

○ **Action item:** What are the core responsibilities (personal and spiritual) of this season in your life that are important for you to persist in doing even when you feel pulled down with grief?

How does persisting in these responsibilities reveal faith?

WHAT TIME I AM AFRAID, I WILL TRUST IN THEE. IN GOD I WILL PRAISE HIS WORD, IN GOD I HAVE PUT MY TRUST; I WILL NOT FEAR WHAT FLESH CAN DO UNTO ME. (PSALM 56:3–4)

TRUSTING GOD'S FAITHFULNESS

WHEN I FEEL AFRAID

Session Notes

Discussion

Devotional Readings

1. Taking Our Fears to God
2. The Abraham Moment
3. God Is Greater
4. Watch and Pray
5. Light for the Journey

Personal Application

TRUSTING GOD'S FAITHFULNESS

*"Be merciful unto me, O God: for man would swallow me up; he fighting daily oppresseth
me.2 Mine enemies would daily swallow me up: for they be many that fight against me,
O thou most High.3 What time I am afraid, I will trust in thee.4 In God I will praise his
word, in God I have put my trust; I will not fear what flesh can do unto me.5 Every day
they wrest my words: all their thoughts are against me for evil.6 They gather themselves
together, they hide themselves, they mark my steps, when they wait for my soul.7 Shall
they escape by iniquity? in thine anger cast down the people, O God.8 Thou tellest my
wanderings: put thou my tears into thy bottle: are they not in thy book?9 When I cry
unto thee, then shall mine enemies turn back: this I know; for God is for me.10 In God
will I praise his word: in the LORD will I praise his word.11 In God have I put my trust:
I will not be afraid what man can do unto me." (Psalm 56:1–11)*

INTRODUCTION

____

____

____

1. THE ____________________ OF FEAR

*"Be merciful unto me, O God: for man would swallow me up; he fighting daily
oppresseth me. 2 Mine enemies would daily swallow me up: for they be many that
fight against me, O thou most High." (Psalm 56:1–2)*

- **Fear of Grief Itself**

  *"God is our refuge and strength, a very present help in trouble. 2 Therefore will not
  we fear, though the earth be removed, and though the mountains be carried into
  the midst of the sea; 3 Though the waters thereof roar and be troubled, though the
  mountains shake with the swelling thereof. Selah." (Psalm 46:1–3)*

- **Fear of Death**

  "We are confident, I say, and willing rather to be absent from the body, and to be present with the Lord." (2 Corinthians 5:8)

- **Situational Fears**

  "Fear thou not; for I am with thee: be not dismayed; for I am thy God: I will strengthen thee; yea, I will help thee; yea, I will uphold thee with the right hand of my righteousness." (Isaiah 41:10)

- **Fear of the Future**

  "And the LORD, he it is that doth go before thee; he will be with thee, he will not fail thee, neither forsake thee: fear not, neither be dismayed." (Deuteronomy 31:8)

- **Fears Related to Your Relationship with God**

  "Yea, though I walk through the valley of the shadow of death, I will fear no evil: for thou art with me; thy rod and thy staff they comfort me." (Psalm 23:4)

"What time I am afraid, I will trust in thee." (Psalm 56:3)

2. THE decision OF TRUST

A choice

"Wait on the LORD: be of good courage, and he shall strengthen thine heart: wait, I say, on the LORD." (Psalm 27:14)

"The LORD is my strength and my shield; my heart trusted in him, and I am helped: therefore my heart greatly rejoiceth; and with my song will I praise him." (Psalm 28:7)

"In God I will praise his word, in God I have put my trust; I will not fear what flesh can do unto me." (Psalm 56:4)

"In God will I praise his word: in the LORD will I praise his word." (Psalm 56:10)

"My heart is fixed, O God, my heart is fixed: I will sing and give praise." (Psalm 57:7)

"The law of the LORD is perfect, converting the soul: the testimony of the LORD is sure, making wise the simple. 8 The statutes of the LORD are right, rejoicing the heart: the commandment of the LORD is pure, enlightening the eyes. 9 The fear of the LORD is clean, enduring for ever: the judgments of the LORD are true and righteous altogether." (Psalm 19:7–9)

Quote: *"What did this book mean to me during the long and weary years of solitary confinement and then for the last four years at Dachau? The Word of God was simply everything to me—comfort and strength, guidance and hope, master of my days and companion of my nights, the bread which kept me from starvation and the water of life that refreshed my soul."*—**Martin Neimöller**

A CONVICTION

*"Shall they escape by iniquity? in thine anger cast down the people, O God. . . .
9 When I cry unto thee, then shall mine enemies turn back: this I know; for God is
for me."* (Psalm 56:7, 9)

"And God is able to make all grace abound toward you; that ye, always having all sufficiency in all things, may abound to every good work:" (2 Corinthians 9:8)

"Thou tellest my wanderings: put thou my tears into thy bottle: are they not in thy book?" (Psalm 56:8)

"And when he had taken the book, the four beasts and four and twenty elders fell down before the Lamb, having every one of them harps, and golden vials full of odours, which are the prayers of saints." (Revelation 5:8)

3. THE CONFIDENCE OF FAITH

*"When I cry unto thee, then shall mine enemies turn back: this I know; for God
is for me. 10 In God will I praise his word: in the LORD will I praise his word.
11 In God have I put my trust: I will not be afraid what man can do unto me."*
(Psalm 56:9–11)

"The LORD is on my side; I will not fear: what can man do unto me?" (Psalm 118:6)

*"What shall we then say to these things? If God be for us, who can be against us?
32 He that spared not his own Son, but delivered him up for us all, how shall he
not with him also freely give us all things?"* (Romans 8:31–32)

- **God is for your salvation.**

  "Herein is love, not that we loved God, but that he loved us, and sent his Son to be the propitiation for our sins." (1 John 4:10)

- **God is for your healing.**

  "He healeth the broken in heart, and bindeth up their wounds." (Psalm 147:3)

- **God is for your growth.**
  "Being confident of this very thing, that he which hath begun a good work in you will perform it until the day of Jesus Christ:" (Philippians 1:6)

CONCLUSION

___

___

___

"In God have I put my trust: I will not be afraid what man can do unto me." (Psalm 56:11)

GROUP DISCUSSION

1. Was there anything from last week's devotionals or application exercises that was particularly meaningful or helpful to you? What passage of Scripture has been most reassuring to you this past week?

2. What are some of the lies that we are tempted to believe when we encounter or struggle with fear (for example, "My faith is weak," or "God isn't near me")? And what are some of the biblical truths that counter these lies?

3. What are some ways Christians can strengthen their confidence in God during a season of grief?

4. What are some of your favorite Bible promises to go to when you feel fear starting to build in your heart?

5. What is one way the group can pray for you as it relates to grief this week?

SESSION SEVEN: DAY ONE

TAKING OUR FEARS TO GOD

What time I am afraid, I will trust in thee. (Psalm 56:3)

The expression "frozen in fear" is descriptive for more reasons than one. Not only does it accurately describe fear's paralyzing effect, but it captures the way that a moment tends to freeze in our memory.

One of those moments for me was when our adult son Larry called to tell me that he had cancer. He had asked his doctor a few weeks prior about an unusual symptom he was experiencing. The doctor ordered a test just to be sure, but both of them assumed it was nothing. The lab delayed, and Larry was surprised when he got a call from his doctor weeks later. It was cancer, and they wanted him in for surgery—and fast.

Just the word *cancer* coming from my own son struck fear into my heart. And if I live to be one hundred, I'll never forget what it was like to see Larry after a surgery that left him with fifty-six staples in his abdomen. Nor will I forget the excruciating pain that followed, with complications requiring yet another surgery followed by rounds of chemotherapy.

These were challenging and, yes, sometimes dark days for our family. I had never known what it was to live day after day within gripping distance of fear. Some days, it seemed like fear won.

I remember on one of those days calling my friend, a longtime pastor in another state, and telling him, "R. B., sometimes I feel like such a weak Christian to be struggling with fear like this." He must have silently asked the Lord for words, because his answer was just what I needed to hear. He told me that there is no sin in being afraid; the sin, rather, is in failing to take our fears to God when we do feel fear. After all, David himself said, "What time I am afraid, I will trust in thee" (Psalm 56:3)—not *if*, but *when* I am afraid... I will choose to trust.

Although I still felt fear after that conversation, I also felt confidence that every time I brought my fear to God, making the choice to trust Him despite the circumstances, I was exercising faith. You see, victory over fear does not come from not having anything to fear, but from reckoning that God can be trusted with our fear.

Fear in times of grief can be overwhelming. Paralyzing. Consuming. But here is the good news: we don't have to be controlled by fear. We may sometimes feel fear, but as we take our fears to Christ, we can rest in the arms of the one who holds us firmly in His grasp and will never let go (John 10:28–29).

TODAY'S TAKEAWAY

When fears enter our lives, we exercise faith by choosing to trust God with our fears by bringing them to Him in prayer.

JOURNAL PROMPT

Were there any areas of fear mentioned in this week's group session that you particularly identify with? Or are there any other areas of fear that you have noticed you are struggling with? Take this opportunity to bring those fears to the Lord and to ask Him to fill your heart with "the peace of God, which passeth all understanding" (Philippians 4:7).

SESSION SEVEN: DAY TWO

THE ABRAHAM MOMENT

In God have I put my trust. (Psalm 56:11)

As I mentioned in our last devotion, I remember like it was yesterday when our oldest son was diagnosed with cancer. For the first months of his treatment, it seemed like every report was negative. He had to have two extensive surgeries, and both brought serious complications. Then, in his already-weakened condition, he had to start chemo.

These challenges brought a great fear of the future into my heart. While discussing Larry's health in another conversation with my friend R. B., he asked me a question that I frankly didn't want to hear: "Have you ever had an 'Abraham moment' when you completely yielded Larry to the Lord?"

I knew that he was referring to when Abraham surrendered to God's will in bringing his son Isaac to Mount Moriah to offer him to the Lord. This was a moment of total surrender to God's will in Abraham's life. But although I understood the question, I didn't know how to answer it. I wanted to sound godly and say, "Of course, whatever God wants is what I want." But I hadn't had that moment and wasn't even sure I could or wanted to.

A day or two later, Terrie and I were in our kitchen talking, as usual, about Larry and, also as usual, crying. I mentioned the question our friend had posed about an "Abraham moment" and asked Terrie, "Have *you* had that moment?" I'm not sure what I expected her to say. Although Terrie is often a stronger Christian than I am, I think I wanted her to tell me that the question was irrational and that God would never expect us to fully release Larry to Him like that. But Terrie didn't flinch. "I have," she said. "I pray that God heals our son, but I told Him I trust Him to do what is best."

Terrie's faith strengthened me to yield Larry and the outcome of his cancer battle to the Lord, fully trusting that He would do what was best.

In our case, God did heal Larry, and we thank Him every day for it. But I don't think I'll ever forget the excruciating pain of coming to that point of complete trust—my "Abraham moment." And I have gone back to this need for surrender to God in other instances of uncertainty and grief. God has not always answered the way I have hoped, but He has always done what is right.

Growing in trust through grief will require surrender. And arriving at that point of total surrender will almost certainly be painful. There are no guarantees that God will miraculously intervene in our circumstances in the way we might wish. The fact is, we don't know why God chooses to bring healing in some cases but not in others.

In the end, however, the thing that *is* guaranteed—what God has always promised His people (Deuteronomy 31:6)—is His continued presence and the blessings of a more resilient faith. And *that* is a promise we can depend on.

TODAY'S TAKEAWAY

We can always trust our loving Heavenly Father with the people and dreams which we hold most dear. We can put our trust in Him because He loves us.

JOURNAL PROMPT

What is the one thing you most fear losing as you go through this season of grief? Have you, like Abraham, surrendered that thing you love to God? Talk with God honestly about this fear, and write a prayer of surrender to Him here.

SESSION SEVEN: DAY THREE

GOD IS GREATER

These things I have spoken unto you, that in me ye might have peace. In the world ye shall have tribulation: but be of good cheer; I have overcome the world. (John 16:33)

Fear is a natural and normal response to things that we are apprehensive about—especially perceived dangers. The problem with fear, however, is that it can warp our perspective. Fear sees the obstacles instead of the possibilities, and it makes the obstacles appear bigger than they really are.

Consider the famous story of David and Goliath recounted in 1 Samuel 17. King Saul and the Israeli army were looking at Goliath and wondering how God could help. David was looking to God and wondering how Goliath could stand a chance. What was the difference? Faith.

Fear sees the obstacle, but faith sees the victory. While the rest of the men ran to hide, "David spake to the men that stood by him, saying, What shall be done to the man that killeth this Philistine, and taketh away the reproach from Israel? for who is this uncircumcised Philistine, that he should defy the armies of the living God?" (1 Samuel 17:26).

You and I serve a living God too. Yes, we live in a fallen world with real challenges and real threats that make our hearts tremble. We face unknown and uncertain outcomes. But whatever fear we face, God is greater.

This truth doesn't mean that our worst fears won't be realized. Even godly Job wrote, "For the thing which I greatly feared is come upon me, and that which I was afraid of is come unto me" (Job 3:25). We live in a sin-cursed world, and we encounter heart-breaking griefs.

God has not promised us health, wealth, and nonstop prosperity. But He has promised us His presence. If you know Christ as your Savior, you serve a living God who abides in you and gives you victory to rise above the onslaught of fear. "These things I have spoken unto you, that in me ye might have peace. In the world ye shall have tribulation: but be of good cheer; I have overcome the world" (John 16:33).

Because Jesus has overcome this sin-cursed world and all the fearful things that it contains, we who know Christ need not be shattered or overwhelmed by the circumstances or pressures in which we find ourselves. We do not need to live controlled by the what ifs of tomorrow or the uncertainties of the future. "For God hath not given us the spirit of fear; but of power, and of love, and of a sound mind" (2 Timothy 1:7).

Ultimately, being consumed by fear and walking in faith are incompatible. Fear will cancel out faith, or faith will cancel out fear. We may *feel* fear, but we can *choose* faith. Eventually, that choice will overcome our fear. As our confidence in God grows, we can then say, "Behold, God is my salvation; I will trust, and not be afraid" (Isaiah 12:2).

TODAY'S TAKEAWAY

When the world is collapsing around you, remember that your God is greater than any circumstances you face and the fears they evoke.

JOURNAL PROMPT

Think about a few of the attributes of God as revealed in Scripture—for example, His omnipotence and omniscience, or the fact that He is loving and just. Then, for each trait you've identified, list one way that trait makes God "greater" than your fears. Write your responses here.

Example: Because God is omniscient, He is able to direct my steps.

SESSION SEVEN: DAY FOUR

WATCH AND PRAY

Watch and pray, that ye enter not into temptation. (Matthew 26:41)

It was a tired, weary group of men who entered the Garden of Gethsemane on the night Jesus was betrayed. Jesus and His disciples had just enjoyed a Passover meal together—a special time, but one filled with bittersweetness: He predicted that one of their own would betray Him, a proclamation that brought sorrow and sadness (Matthew 26:22).

During that time in the garden, Jesus prayed fervently to His Father, asking that the "cup" of suffering might pass Him by but then immediately saying, "nevertheless not as I will, but as thou wilt" (Matthew 26:39). This provides a model for us in our prayers: request for relief of suffering coupled with humble submission to the will of a Father who truly knows what is best for us and for the world He created.

While in the Garden of Gethsemane, Jesus also issued three directives to his disciples that are instructive to us as we journey through our own seasons of grief and distress.

First, He asked His disciples to "Sit ye here, while I go and pray yonder" (Matthew 26:36). *Sit. Stay still. Remain calm.* These are not easy things to do when our world is crashing down around us. But this is exactly what He asked His disciples to do—and it's what He asks of us as well.

Next, Jesus took Peter, James, and John with him and withdrew a bit from the rest of the disciples. To these three, Jesus gave this command: "tarry ye here, and watch with me" (Matthew 26:38). Don't just sit still—*be vigilant*.

But what were they to watch for? Jesus' third and final command answers this question. After moving on about a stone's throw from the disciples, Jesus spent an hour in prayer with His Father. He then returned to where He had left Peter, James, and John—only to find them sleeping. Singling Peter out specifically, Jesus asked, "What, could ye not watch with me one hour? Watch and pray, that ye enter not into temptation" (Matthew 26:40–41). Be vigilant against temptation—and use prayer to combat it. *Watch... and pray*.

Like the disciples, we too must pray that we do not succumb to temptation in the midst of our season of grief, fear, and anxiety. For us, the temptation may be to give up hope, to give in to despair, to turn our focus inward and sink in self-pity. It may be the temptation to walk away from responsibilities or relationships to which we have long been committed. Or it may be the temptation to drown our sorrows in unhealthy and harmful behaviors. Whatever the temptation may be, our Lord urges us to pray that we might remain vigilant and watchful against that temptation. And the good news, as 1 Corinthians 10:13 assures us, is that no temptation has overtaken us "but such as is common to man." In such cases, "God is faithful, who will not suffer [us] to be tempted above that [we] are able; but will with the temptation also make a way to escape, that [we] may be able to bear it."

TODAY'S TAKEAWAY

Take time to sit in the Lord's presence, watch and wait for His guidance, and pray for protection from temptation.

JOURNAL PROMPT

What are some of the specific or repeated temptations you find yourself facing in this journey of grief? Jot down any that come to mind, and write a prayer asking the Lord to protect you from those temptations and to give you the strength to resist them.

Session 7: Day 5

SESSION SEVEN: DAY FIVE

LIGHT FOR THE JOURNEY

Thy word is a lamp unto my feet, and a light unto my path. (Psalm 119:105)

We learned in this week's group session that when David found himself in the grip of fear, he made two simple choices: to trust in the Lord and to praise His Word.

But what is it, exactly, that makes God's Word praiseworthy? Here are four reasons we can praise God for His Word:

Scripture is *necessary* for understanding God Himself. As 1 Corinthians 2:6–13 explains, no one except the Spirit of God knows the mind of God and the things He has planned for us (verse 9). The Spirit reveals these things to us (verse 10), and one of the ways He does this is through the words of the Bible. We need Scripture because we need to know God.

Scripture is *sufficient* for our every need. "All scripture is given by inspiration of God, and is profitable for doctrine, for reproof, for correction, for instruction in righteousness: That the man of God may be perfect, thoroughly furnished unto all good works" (2 Timothy 3:16–17).

Scripture is *clear* and provides needed clarity for our lives. As Moses was preparing the people of Israel to enter the Promised Land, he reiterated God's laws for them and then said that "this commandment which I command thee this day, it is not hidden from thee, neither is it far off . . . the word is very nigh unto thee, in thy mouth, and in thy heart, that thou mayest do it" (Deuteronomy 30:11–14).

Scripture is *authoritative*. Psalm 138:2 tells us that God has exalted His Word even above His already-great reputation: ". . . thou hast magnified thy word above all thy name." When we acknowledge the authority God's Word in our lives, we cannot help but praise the one from whom that Word came: God Himself.

What does all this have to do with us on our journey of grief? As it turns out, everything! We are absolutely dependent on God's Word for successfully navigating our journey through grief.

- When the path ahead of us is dark and stormy, it is necessary that we know God's heart for us, His children. We get to know His heart in the pages of His Word.
- God's Word is sufficient to fight our fears. As we travel along the road of grief, we can use the promises of Scripture as a sword to fight back the onslaught of anxiety and worry (Ephesians 6:17).
- God's Word provides the clarity we need in confusing times. When we can't see the path in front of us, we can find much-needed guidance and hope in the Scriptures.
- When our world is crashing down around us, the authority of God's Word provides an anchor for our souls. Though the strong winds come blowing, our spiritual "house" will stand because it is built on a firm foundation (Matthew 7:24–27).

The necessity, sufficiency, clarity, and authority of God's Word work together to provide us with illumination for our journey. As the psalmist puts it, "Thy word is a lamp unto my feet, and a light unto my path" (Psalm 119:105). We may see only one step ahead of us on the road, but we can rest assured that God's Word will never lead us astray.

TODAY'S TAKEAWAY

As we walk the path of grief, we can rest assured that God's Word will give us the help that we need.

JOURNAL PROMPT

What are some specific ways in which the Word of God has been helpful to you in this season of grief?

PERSONAL APPLICATION

The following exercises are intended to give you an opportunity to apply the things you're learning and discussing in the group meetings and daily devotionals. They don't have to be done in any particular sequence or on a particular day of the week. If you only have the physical or emotional energy to complete one of these exercises, that's fine. The point is to allow the Spirit of God to minister to your heart during this time of grief.

MAKING DECISIONS OF TRUST

The key to keeping our fears from controlling our lives is to make conscious "decisions of trust" in response to them. When fears arise in our hearts, we can ask ourselves, "What would a decision of trust look like in this particular moment of fear?"

- **Action Item:** Look back at your journal entry for Session 3, Day 1, in which you listed some of the specific fears with which you were struggling at that time. Are you still experiencing those same fears? Have new or different ones arisen since then? Make a list of the fears (new or old) that you're currently experiencing. Then, for each fear, write out a concrete decision of trust that you can make this week that will help shift your focus from fear to trust in God.

  For instance, if you feel afraid as you go to bed at night without your spouse, what can you do to remind yourself of God's presence and focus your trust in Him? It might be that you would go to sleep listening to an audio Bible recording. It might be that you would sing hymns of praise as you get ready for bed. It might be that you would call a friend and pray together on the phone. Whatever it is, planning specific ways you can turn your focus from your fear to trust in the moments of fear will help to grow your faith.

For each of the fears you identified above, complete the following sentences:

I am currently experiencing fear of . . .

The concrete decision of trust I can make to shift my focus from fear to trust in God is . . .

____

____

____

DEVELOPING ROUTINES OF FAITH

One of the most significant ways to nurture our faith is by daily spending time with the Lord—reading His Word and bringing our needs to Him in prayer. Of course, we can pray and read the Bible at any point during the day. But developing the habit of a daily set time ensures we do it every day. Making it a habit also helps build our faith in incremental steps as we seek God's face day by day.

Consistent prayer and devotional practices anchor us in God's presence, providing a refuge from the turmoil of grief and anxiety. These routines foster a deeper relationship with the Lord, allowing us to draw strength and comfort from His promises and to pour out our hearts to Him in prayer.

○ **Action item:** Take a few minutes to consider your daily devotional habits. Are you consistently getting dedicated time to read God's Word and pray? Are there ways you would like to freshen up this time? Use the prompts below to make plans that will help you grow in this practice.

My daily devotional time is/will be . . . ____________________

My devotional plan is to read . . . ____________________

I want to change up what I'm currently doing in this way . . . ____________________

____

STABILIZING YOUR SOUL

In Psalm 1, we are told that the believer who takes delight in God's Word and meditates on it "day and night" is "blessed" (Psalm 1:1–2). This observation is followed by an incredible promise: the person who meditates on God's law "shall be like a tree planted by the rivers of water, that bringeth forth his fruit in his season; his leaf also shall not wither" (Psalm 1:3). Meditating on God's Word is a key to strength, endurance, and continued fruitfulness, especially in times of grief.

Writing out the words of Scripture can help us meditate on it, which in turn can help to internalize and apply it. When our souls are rocked by the stormy waves of grief, meditating on God's Word can help to stabilize them.

O **Action item:** Pick one of the following three passages of Scripture that we looked at this week:

- Psalm 56:3–4
- Isaiah 41:10
- Psalm 28:7

(Or, if some other passage of Scripture has been particularly meaningful to you this week, pick that one.)

Next, write out the passage in the space provided here.

Finally, if you haven't done so already, memorize the passage and use it as a basis for meditation and prayer throughout this week.

AND HE SAID UNTO ME, MY GRACE IS SUFFICIENT FOR THEE: FOR MY STRENGTH IS MADE PERFECT IN WEAKNESS. MOST GLADLY THEREFORE WILL I RATHER GLORY IN MY INFIRMITIES, THAT THE POWER OF CHRIST MAY REST UPON ME. (2 CORINTHIANS 12:9)

EMBRACING GOD'S GRACE

WHEN I FEEL WEAK

Session Notes

Discussion

Devotional Readings

1. A Strange Companion
2. Grace in the Gaps
3. The Purification of Faith
4. Faith in the Furnace
5. Grace for Today

Personal Application

EMBRACING GOD'S GRACE

*"It is not expedient for me doubtless to glory. I will come to visions and revelations of
the Lord.2 I knew a man in Christ above fourteen years ago, (whether in the body, I
cannot tell; or whether out of the body, I cannot tell: God knoweth;) such an one caught
up to the third heaven.3 And I knew such a man, (whether in the body, or out of the
body, I cannot tell: God knoweth;)4 How that he was caught up into paradise, and heard
unspeakable words, which it is not lawful for a man to utter.5 Of such an one will I
glory: yet of myself I will not glory, but in mine infirmities.6 For though I would desire
to glory, I shall not be a fool; for I will say the truth: but now I forbear, lest any man
should think of me above that which he seeth me to be, or that he heareth of me.7 And
lest I should be exalted above measure through the abundance of the revelations, there
was given to me a thorn in the flesh, the messenger of Satan to buffet me, lest I should be
exalted above measure.8 For this thing I besought the Lord thrice, that it might depart
from me.9 And he said unto me, My grace is sufficient for thee: for my strength is made
perfect in weakness. Most gladly therefore will I rather glory in my infirmities, that
the power of Christ may rest upon me.10 Therefore I take pleasure in infirmities, in
reproaches, in necessities, in persecutions, in distresses for Christ's sake: for when I am
weak, then am I strong." (2 Corinthians 12:1–10)*

INTRODUCTION

WHEN I Feel weak

"But the God of all grace, who hath called us unto his eternal glory by Christ Jesus, after that ye have suffered a while, make you perfect, stablish, strengthen, settle you."(1 Peter 5:10)

*"For by grace are ye saved through faith; and that not of yourselves: it is the gift of God:
9 Not of works, lest any man should boast." (Ephesians 2:8–9)*

"And God is able to make all grace abound toward you; that ye, always having all sufficiency in all things, may abound to every good work:" (2 Corinthians 9:8)

*"And lest I should be exalted above measure through the abundance of the revelations, there was given to me a thorn in the flesh, the messenger of Satan to buffet me, lest I
should be exalted above measure. 8 For this thing I besought the Lord thrice, that it*

might depart from me. 9 And he said unto me, My grace is sufficient for thee: for my strength is made perfect in weakness..." (2 Corinthians 12:7–9)

1. Humble BY GRACE

"*It is not expedient for me doubtless to glory. I will come to visions and revelations of the Lord. 2 I knew a man in Christ above fourteen years ago, (whether in the body, I cannot tell; or whether out of the body, I cannot tell: God knoweth;) such an one caught up to the third heaven. 3 And I knew such a man, (whether in the body, or out of the body, I cannot tell: God knoweth;) 4 How that he was caught up into paradise, and heard unspeakable words, which it is not lawful for a man to utter.*" (2 Corinthians 12:1–4)

"*But he giveth more grace. Wherefore he saith, God resisteth the proud, but giveth grace unto the humble.*" (James 4:6)

Grief Is an going Pain

"*And lest I should be exalted above measure through the abundance of the revelations, there was given to me a thorn in the flesh, the messenger of Satan to buffet me, lest I should be exalted above measure.*" (2 Corinthians 12:7)

"*Ye know how through infirmity of the flesh I preached the gospel unto you at the first. 14 And my temptation which was in my flesh ye despised not, nor rejected; but received me as an angel of God, even as Christ Jesus. 15 Where is then the blessedness ye spake of? for I bear you record, that, if it had been possible, ye would have plucked out your own eyes, and have given them to me.*" (Galatians 4:13–15)

Definition: *Buffet*—"to strike with the fist, give one a blow with the fist; to maltreat, treat with violence."

Grace Is a continual Gift

"*And lest I should be exalted above measure through the abundance of the revelations, there was given to me a thorn in the flesh, the messenger of Satan to buffet me, lest I should be exalted above measure.*" (2 Corinthians 12:7)

"*The LORD is nigh unto them that are of a broken heart; and saveth such as be of a contrite spirit.*" (Psalm 34:18)

"*For this thing I besought the Lord thrice, that it might depart from me.*" (2 Corinthians 12:8)

THREE PRAYER REQUESTS FOR A SEASON OF GRIEF

1. *God's Will*

"And he was withdrawn from them about a stone's cast, and kneeled
down, and prayed, 42 Saying, Father, if thou be willing, remove
this cup from me: nevertheless not my will, but thine, be done."
(Luke 22:41–42)

"And this is the confidence that we have in him, that, if we ask any
thing according to his will, he heareth us:" (1 John 5:14)

2. *Wisdom*

"If any of you lack wisdom, let him ask of God, that giveth to all men
liberally, and upbraideth not; and it shall be given him." (James 1:5)

3. *Comfort*

"Now our Lord Jesus Christ himself, and God, even our Father,
which hath loved us, and hath given us everlasting consolation and
good hope through grace, 17 Comfort your hearts, and stablish you
in every good word and work." (2 Thessalonians 2:16–17)

2. ___strenghten___ BY GRACE

Grief ___reveal___ Our Weakness

"I am verily a man which am a Jew, born in Tarsus, a city in Cilicia, yet brought up in this city at the feet of Gamaliel, and taught according to the perfect manner of the law of the fathers, and was zealous toward God, as ye all are this day." (Acts 22:3)

*"Though I might also have confidence in the flesh. If any other man thinketh that
he hath whereof he might trust in the flesh, I more: 5 Circumcised the eighth
day, of the stock of Israel, of the tribe of Benjamin, an Hebrew of the Hebrews; as
touching the law, a Pharisee; 6 Concerning zeal, persecuting the church; touching
the righteousness which is in the law, blameless." (Philippians 3:4–6)*

"But what things were gain to me, those I counted loss for Christ." (Philippians 3:7)

*"Hast thou not known? hast thou not heard, that the everlasting God, the LORD,
the Creator of the ends of the earth, fainteth not, neither is weary? there is no
searching of his understanding. 29 He giveth power to the faint; and to them that
have no might he increaseth strength. 30 Even the youths shall faint and be weary,
and the young men shall utterly fall: 31 But they that wait upon the LORD shall
renew their strength; they shall mount up with wings as eagles; they shall run, and
not be weary; and they shall walk, and not faint." (Isaiah 40:28–31)*

Grace delivers God's Strength

"And he said unto me, My grace is sufficient for thee: for my strength is made perfect in weakness. Most gladly therefore will I rather glory in my infirmities, that the power of Christ may rest upon me." (2 Corinthians 12:9)

"For which cause we faint not; but though our outward man perish, yet the inward man is renewed day by day." (2 Corinthians 4:16)

3. Purifies BY GRACE

*"Knowing this, that the trying of your faith worketh patience. 4 But let patience
have her perfect work, that ye may be perfect and entire, wanting nothing."
(James 1:3–4)*

Defintion: *is made perfect,* from *teleioō*— "to complete, to perfect; to carry through completely, to accomplish, finish, bring to an end."

Grief ~~exposes~~ exposes Our Need

*"For ye see your calling, brethren, how that not many wise men after the flesh, not
many mighty, not many noble, are called: 27 But God hath chosen the foolish
things of the world to confound the wise; and God hath chosen the weak things
of the world to confound the things which are mighty; 28 And base things of the
world, and things which are despised, hath God chosen, yea, and things which
are not, to bring to nought things that are: 29 That no flesh should glory in his
presence." (1 Corinthians 1:26–29)*

Grace purify Our Faith

"But he knoweth the way that I take: when he hath tried me, I shall come forth as gold." (Job 23:10)

"Moreover the LORD answered Job, and said, 2 Shall he that contendeth with the Almighty instruct him? he that reproveth God, let him answer it. 3 Then Job answered the LORD, and said, 4 Behold, I am vile; what shall I answer thee? I will lay mine hand upon my mouth." (Job 40:1–4)*

"That the trial of your faith, being much more precious than of gold that perisheth, though it be tried with fire, might be found unto praise and honour and glory at the appearing of Jesus Christ:" (1 Peter 1:7)

4. Empowered BY GRACE

"...Most gladly therefore will I rather glory in my infirmities, that the power of Christ may rest upon me." (2 Corinthians 12:9)

Grief deflates Our Energy

Grace enables Our Progress

"...Most gladly therefore will I rather glory in my infirmities, that the power of Christ may rest upon me. 10 Therefore I take pleasure in infirmities, in reproaches, in necessities, in persecutions, in distresses for Christ's sake: for when I am weak, then am I strong." (2 Corinthians 12:9–10)

CONCLUSION

GROUP DISCUSSION

1. Was there anything from last week's devotionals or application exercises that was particularly meaningful or helpful to you? What passage of Scripture has been most reassuring to you this past week?

2. The Bible tells us that God uses our weaknesses to reveal our need for Him. If you feel comfortable doing so, share with the group one or more areas in which you feel weak during this season. How is God using that area of weakness to show you His strength?

3. What are some of the means God, by His grace, uses to give us His strength?

4. Who have you observed over the years receiving God's grace in the midst of their grief? How has their testimony been an encouragement to you?

5. What is one way the group can pray for you as it relates to grief this week? (A prayer request section is included at the end of this workbook so you can record the requests of other group members.)

SESSION EIGHT: DAY ONE

A STRANGE COMPANION

And he said unto me, My grace is sufficient for thee: for my strength is made perfect in weakness. (2 Corinthians 12:9)

After more than forty years living as a quadriplegic, Joni Eareckson Tada faced a new challenge: chronic physical pain. Unrelenting, grinding, constant pain. The kind of pain that seeps into the very depths of your being and makes it hard to breathe. The kind of pain that simply doesn't stop. The kind that makes you yearn for Heaven.

Having already learned so much from decades of life as a quadriplegic, Joni set out to record what the Lord was now teaching her through her struggle with chronic pain. The result, a book titled *A Place of Healing*, explores the mystery of how pain and suffering mesh with God's sovereignty in a broken world. Along the way, Joni shares her insights regarding the spiritual benefits of pain in the believer's life and offers counsel for those who can't imagine how they can persevere in the face of persistent pain and suffering.

Just after completing this book manuscript, Joni received yet another blow: the diagnosis of breast cancer. Since then, she's gone through two (successful) battles with cancer, has contracted and recovered from Covid, and has continued to navigate the challenges of living with quadriplegia and chronic pain.

Clearly, Joni's faith has been hard-won. She speaks from a place of personal experience and authority when she says,

> *Pain is a bruising of a blessing, but it is a blessing nonetheless. It's a strange, dark companion, but a companion—if only because it has passed through God's inspecting hand. It's an unwelcome guest, but still a guest. I know that it drives me to a place of nearer, more intimate fellowship with Jesus, and so I take pain as though I were taking the left hand of God. (Better the left hand than no hand at all.)*[1]

As Joni's words suggest, she has come to accept the fact that whatever comes into her life, it has done so only because God has permitted it for His good reasons—to accomplish His perfect will in her life. And what is God's will—not just for Joni but for all of us? It is "that you and I be in the best position, the best place, the timeliest circumstance in which God can be glorified the most."[2]

Of course, this perspective is possible only when our pain and suffering are viewed through the lens of God's grace. It is grace that empowers us to live out God's will for us even when it involves pain and suffering. And it is grace that enables us to say of our own journey through grief, "This, too, will glorify God"—even when we can't see how that could possibly be the case.

Pain of any variety—whether physical, emotional, or spiritual—is a "strange companion" indeed. It is never pleasant. But it can be a blessing when we allow it to press us into the embrace of our loving Father who holds us in His arms, and whose hands filter everything that comes our way.

TODAY'S TAKEAWAY

When we rely on God's grace in the midst of our pain and weakness, His strength becomes our strength, and He is glorified.

JOURNAL PROMPT

Do you find your heart crying out, "Lord, your grace doesn't feel sufficient for me today"? Tell the Lord about those areas where you desire to experience the grace that He offers.

SESSION EIGHT: DAY TWO

GRACE IN THE GAPS

But we have this treasure in earthen vessels, that the excellency of the power may be of God, and not of us. (2 Corinthians 4:7)

The ancient Japanese people developed a method of restoring broken pottery that has become an art form in its own right and is a perfect illustration of how God's grace works in our weaknesses to display His glory. Known as *kintsugi*, this method involves putting pieces of broken ceramic back together again, using fillings of gold, silver, or platinum.[3] What results from this process is an artifact that simultaneously retains certain characteristics of the original, unbroken ceramic while also taking on new characteristics. In the end, the restored work possesses an even greater beauty than it had originally, reflecting the painstaking restorative and creative work done by the artist.

Grief humbles us. It can make us feel weak. Broken. We can feel like we've been shattered into a million pieces, never to be put back together again.

But we serve a master Artist—God Himself—who loves us and is working to bring healing and restoration in our lives even when we can't see His hand at work.

As God gently does His creative work in our lives, He provides strength—His strength—where we are weak. His grace heals the broken places in our lives and puts them back together. Sometimes quickly, often slowly, carefully, methodically. But we are never the same as we were before He began His work in us: the signs of His craftsmanship remain with us forever.

In the process of putting our broken pieces back together, the master Artist focuses on the purpose for which we were created: to put God's glory on display. Second Corinthians 4:7 tells us that we have within us a treasure—the "gospel of Christ . . . the light of the knowledge of the glory of God in the face of Jesus Christ" (2 Corinthians 4:4, 6)—that is intended to shine for the world to see. And yet, as Joni Eareckson Tada has observed, "if our very life purpose is to display the treasure we contain within, that display often works best when there are faults and cracks and chips in the pot! It is through these that the radiant, resplendent glory of Jesus shines through to the wondering eyes of the world."[4]

What does this mean for us during our season of grief? Just like the pieces of ceramic that are restored by the *kintsugi* artist, our lives will show the marks of God's sustaining grace. He will have put us back together, but He will have done so in a way that displays *His* power at work in our weaknesses. The result will be a thing of beauty.

God allows us to catch glimpses of that beauty even now—even in grief. And sometimes we see it more fully as the years go by. But ultimately, we will more fully see what God, the Master Artist, has done when we enter eternity and are fully conformed to the beautiful image of Christ.

TODAY'S TAKEAWAY

No matter how weak, frail, broken, or unusable we may feel right now, we can rest assured that God *will* bring healing and restoration to our lives. He will put the pieces back together.

JOURNAL PROMPT

In what ways can you see God filling you in with "gold" to make you stronger? Take a moment to thank Him for the work He is doing in your life.

SESSION EIGHT: DAY THREE

THE PURIFICATION OF FAITH

That the trial of your faith, being much more precious than of gold that perisheth, though it be tried with fire, might be found unto praise and honour and glory at the appearing of Jesus Christ. (1 Peter 1:7)

My mother was a classy lady. She had great taste in clothing and usually wore jewelry with it. She always looked beautifully appropriate for any occasion. It was no surprise then that when Mom died, our only sister, Lis, wanted all of her jewelry.

Lis primarily wanted the jewelry to remember our mother as she wore it. Even so, she got the diamond pieces appraised. What she found out, however, was that all of the diamonds in Mom's jewelry were fake. They looked real, but they were only made for show.

Faith can be the same way. What seems to be a strong, vibrant faith can turn out in fact to be shallow and weak. If we have in faith trusted Christ as our Savior, we can rest assured that our eternal destiny is secure. But that faith, real as it is, is not necessarily mature. For *that*, our faith needs to be tested or "tried" (in the words of 1 Peter 1:7). We need our faith to be purified if we are to grow in the Lord. Grief is sometimes part of that process.

Missionary Gracia Burnham shares a testimony that illustrates this. Gracia and her husband Martin were missionaries to the Philippines but were taken captive and held hostage by terrorists for over a year. In the chaos of a rescue attempt, Martin was shot in the chest and died. Gracia survived but had to face life without her husband.

Over the years since her ordeal in the Philippine jungle, Gracia Burnham has been asked to share her story on numerous occasions. At a conference in 2021, she shared that during her time in captivity, she began to realize that she was not the person she thought she was. Instead of the "pretty good person" she had previously thought herself to be, she came "face to face with the Gracia I didn't want to see"—a hateful, covetous, despairing, and faithless Gracia. She hated her captors for the pain they were causing them and their family. As they all faced starvation, she coveted what little food the terrorists had to eat. And she had all but given up hope: "Nobody cares about us anymore; this has gone on for so long; everyone's forgotten us." As she looked at herself, Gracia concluded, "I was a mess, and it was shocking."

Gracia shared this revelation with her husband, who wisely responded by saying, "Love, joy, peace. Those aren't things you can just make happen in your own heart. Those are gifts from the Holy Spirit of God. Let's ask for them." And so, they did. And, with time, they found that what they couldn't bring about in their hearts by their own effort, the Spirit of God did in and through them: "As we got to know the guys holding us, as we learned their stories, as we saw their spiritual lostness, as we saw their end, my heart began to change towards them. My hatred turned to love. We began to be concerned about their eternity."[5]

Romans 5:3–4 promises that as we are transformed by and through our tribulations, the result is patience, character, and hope. God uses the fires of tribulation to purify our faith—to show us who we really are, and to develop previously unrealized capacities, such as the ability to forgive and love our enemies. In doing this, He is doing a good work in our lives, even though it may not *feel* "good" at the time.

TODAY'S TAKEAWAY

By purifying our faith, God's grace empowers us to become the persons that God has called us to be—mature, faith-filled followers of Christ who can love and forgive even our enemies.

JOURNAL PROMPT

What "gifts of grace" do you need today—love, joy, peace, forgiveness, etc.—that can only come from the Holy Spirit? Ask Him to fill you with His presence and do His good work in your heart.

SESSION EIGHT: DAY FOUR

FAITH IN THE FURNACE

. . . our God whom we serve is able to deliver us . . . But if not . . . (Daniel 3:17–18)

"Throw them in the fire!" Nebuchadnezzar said. He had erected a golden image and commanded the people to bow down in worship of it. Shadrach, Meshach, and Abednego—faithful members of the Jewish community exiled to Babylon—refused to comply. They would worship Jehovah God, and Him alone.

The king of Babylon, Nebuchadnezzar, was none too pleased about their open rebellion. Infuriated, he ordered that the furnace be heated seven times hotter than it normally was, and that these three men be thrown into the fire. But to his astonishment, after he had thrown them into the blazing furnace, Nebuchadnezzar saw a *fourth* figure—one "like the Son of God" (Daniel 3:25)—walking around in the fire alongside the other men. Calling Shadrach, Meshach, and Abednego out of the furnace, Nebuchadnezzar and his court found that the men were completely unscathed. In response, Nebuchadnezzar praised God, acknowledging that "there is no other God that can deliver after this sort" (Daniel 3:29).

The story of Shadrach, Meshach, and Abednego is familiar enough. But it can be easy to overlook what happened between the initial decree to worship the golden image and the command to throw the men into the fire. After being told of their refusal to worship the image, Nebuchadnezzar gave them another chance to worship the image, backed up with the threat that if they still refused to comply, "ye shall be cast the same hour into the midst of a burning fiery furnace; and who is that God that shall deliver you out of my hands?" (Daniel 3:15).

Read their faith-filled response: "If it be so, our God whom we serve is able to deliver us from the burning fiery furnace, and he will deliver us out of thine hand, O king. But if not, be it known unto thee, O king, that we will not serve thy gods, nor worship the golden image which thou hast set up" (Daniel 3:17–18).

But if not. Some of the hardest words to say, especially in a time of pain or grief. We naturally want to be rescued—immediately. But part of growing through grief means being able to say, with our Lord, "nevertheless not my will, but thine, be done" (Luke 22:42).

One of the hard realities of pain and grief is that often we can't see the *why* behind our suffering. Even more difficult can be the realization that sometimes God allows us to experience profound pain, in part, to demonstrate His power to a watching world.

As we consider the account of Shadrach, Meshach, and Abednego, we have the benefit of knowing "the end of the story"—we know that God rescued them unharmed from the fire. But these men had no idea what would happen. They were facing the very real possibility of an agonizingly painful death. All they knew is that their God was able to rescue them and could do so if He chose. And that was enough for them.

You, too, may not know what rescue is coming, or when. But you can stand in the fire with the God who knows you—and He will be enough for you.

TODAY'S TAKEAWAY

When we find ourselves in the furnace of grief, our Lord walks with us. He may or may not rescue us quickly, or in the way that we would like to be rescued. But He can be trusted to stand with us, protect us, and bring glory to Himself even as the fire rages.

JOURNAL PROMPT

Write a prayer to the Lord expressing your trust in Him regardless of the outcome of your furnace experience.

SESSION EIGHT: DAY FIVE

GRACE FOR TODAY

For which cause we faint not; but though our outward man perish, yet the inward man is renewed day by day. (2 Corinthians 4:16)

The path of grief is hard. It can seem never-ending. We may begin to wonder if we have the strength to make it if the journey continues for another week, month, or year—much less the rest of our lives. Part of the secret to "making it" is understanding that we don't live the next week, month, year, or twenty years of our lives all at once. Instead, we live one day at a time. And in that daily living, we find God's daily grace.

Annie Johnson Flint knew a little something about daily grace. With severe arthritis throughout her body, she undoubtedly struggled to accomplish even basic tasks related to self-care. Yet, she relied on the Lord's strength to empower her to write prolifically, producing many poems and hymns that are beloved by Christ-followers to this day. Human weakness forced her to rely upon divine strength, which made its way into the words she wrote. In that way, she served and blessed many others during her lifetime and beyond. At the end of one of her poems, which she titled "One Day at a Time," Annie wrote these profound words:

> *One day at a time, and the day is His day;*
> *He hath numbered its hours, though they haste or delay.*
> *His grace is sufficient; we walk not alone;*
> *As the day, so the strength that He giveth His own.*

There is a little word in the phrase "My grace is sufficient for thee" (2 Corinthians 12:9) that can give all of us courage, and that is the word *is*. God's grace *is* sufficient—not *was* sufficient, not *will* be sufficient but *is* sufficient. It's in the present tense. It is sufficient for you right now—in this very moment.

For those of us who are walking through grief, God's grace is given one day at a time. We don't get—or need—enough grace for the next twenty years, or even a week, month, or year. Instead, we get the grace that we need for *today*. In the words of 2 Corinthians 4:16, we are "renewed day by day." The power of God delivered by His grace is seen in giving grieving Christians the strength to take one step at a time through the journey of grief.

"If God sends us on strong paths, we are provided strong shoes," Corrie ten Boom once said. The path of grief is indeed a hard one—a "strong" path, in ten Boom's phrasing. But when God calls us on that hard path, He also provides what we need—the "shoes"—to be able to walk it. We walk the path one step at a time each day, and God provides the grace to take each and every one of those steps.

TODAY'S TAKEAWAY

God portions out to us the grace we need for *this* day, and He offers that grace to us on a moment-by-moment basis. Because God's grace is always present tense, it is always sufficient.

JOURNAL PROMPT

In what ways do you feel the need for God's grace today? Lay these areas before the Lord in prayer and ask Him to sustain you on a moment-by-moment basis.

PERSONAL APPLICATION

The following exercises are intended to give you an opportunity to apply the things you're learning and discussing in the group meetings and daily devotionals. They don't have to be done in any particular sequence or on a particular day of the week. If you only have the physical or emotional energy to complete one of these exercises, that's fine. The point is to allow the Spirit of God to minister to your heart during this time of grief.

RECEIVING THE GIFT

Nothing humbles us like grief. During our seasons of loss, we are aware of how little we actually control and how greatly we need the Lord. And, although we don't always think of it in these terms, humility is a gift. When we humble ourselves, we can receive God's grace.

Humility in the midst of grief is no guarantee, however. The opportunity for it is a gift, but choosing to humble ourselves is a choice we must make for ourselves.

○ **Action Item:** Take some time to think about and respond to the following questions:

1. Are there areas of your life in which, in an attempt to maintain a semblance of control, you've become even more controlling—being overly demanding, imposing unrealistic or unfair expectations, and so forth—in your interactions with others or even in your relationship with God?

___

___

2. Are there areas of your life in which you need to surrender control so you can receive the gift of humility and, thereby, the gift of grace as well?

THREE PRAYER REQUESTS FOR A SEASON OF GRIEF

One of the principal ways in which we receive the gift of God's grace with humility is through prayer. In prayer, we are reminded that we are not self-sufficient, that we need God, and that our only reliable source of strength and sustenance is found in the Lord.

Of course, prayer can sometimes be challenging when we are weighed down by the burden of grief. In such times, there are three things for which we can pray with absolute assurance and confidence.

First, we can pray for God's will to be done in all things (Luke 22:41–42; 1 John 5:14). Second, we can pray for wisdom as we work through the choices that must be made during this time (James 1:5). And finally, we can pray for God's comfort and peace as we move forward on our journey of grief (2 Thessalonians 2:16–17).

○ **Action item:** As you reflect on the current circumstances of your life, take some time to bring them before the Lord in prayer, focusing specifically on seeking His will, wisdom, and comfort in relation to those circumstances. Record here your prayer and any insights you gain during your time with the Lord.

1. *The Will of God:* Pray in surrender, asking the Lord for His will to be accomplished in your life generally and in the specific situations you are facing presently.

2. *Wisdom from God:* Ask God for wisdom for every choice you must make during this season of grief.

3. *Comfort from God:* Ask the Lord to fill your heart with His comfort and peace.

STABILIZING YOUR SOUL

Using the words of a psalm or a biblically-saturated hymn or poem in prayer can be powerful medicine for your soul during this season of grief. When you can't come up with the words to say yourself, let others who have gone before you lead the way into the caring presence of your Father.

- O **Action item:** Pray through these words of the well-known hymn "Amazing Grace." There is space provided below to record your reflections.

Amazing Grace
By John Newton

Amazing grace! how sweet the sound,
That saved a wretch; like me!
I once was lost, but now am found,
Was blind, but now I see.

'Twas grace that taught my heart to fear,
And grace my fears relieved;
How precious did that grace appear
The hour I first believed!

Through many dangers, toils, and snares,
I have already come;
'Tis grace hath brought me safe thus far,
And grace will lead me home.

The Lord hath promised good to me,
His word my hope secures;
He will my shield and portion be
As long as life endures.

Yea, when this flesh and heart shall fail,
And mortal life shall cease,
I shall possess within the veil
A life of joy and peace.

The earth shall soon dissolve like snow,
The sun forbear to shine;
But God, who called me here below,
Will be forever mine.

When we've been there ten thousand years,
Bright shining as the sun,
We've no less days to sing God's praise
Than when we first begun.

FOR AS WE HAVE MANY MEMBERS IN ONE BODY, AND ALL MEMBERS HAVE NOT THE SAME OFFICE: 5 SO WE, BEING MANY, ARE ONE BODY IN CHRIST, AND EVERY ONE MEMBERS ONE OF ANOTHER. (ROMANS 12:4–5)

STAYING CONNECTED

WHEN I FEEL ALONE

Session Notes

Discussion

Devotional Readings

1. Come Unto Me
2. What We Need
3. With These Words
4. The Power of Habit
5. Serving as to the Lord

Personal Application

STAYING CONNECTED

*"Then they that gladly received his word were baptized: and the same day there were
added unto them about three thousand souls. 42 And they continued stedfastly in the
apostles' doctrine and fellowship, and in breaking of bread, and in prayers. 43 And
fear came upon every soul: and many wonders and signs were done by the apostles.
44 And all that believed were together, and had all things common; 45 And sold their
possessions and goods, and parted them to all men, as every man had need. 46 And
they, continuing daily with one accord in the temple, and breaking bread from house to
house, did eat their meat with gladness and singleness of heart, 47 Praising God, and
having favour with all the people. And the Lord added to the church daily such as should
be saved." (Acts 2:41–47)*

INTRODUCTION

____

____

____

1. CONNECTED TO Truth

"And they continued stedfastly in the apostles' doctrine . . ." (Acts 2:42)

"And daily in the temple, and in every house, they ceased not to teach and preach Jesus Christ." (Acts 5:42)

"Paul also and Barnabas continued in Antioch, teaching and preaching the word of the Lord, with many others also." (Acts 15:35)

*"And upon the first day of the week, when the disciples came together to break bread,
Paul preached unto them, ready to depart on the morrow; and continued his speech
until midnight. . . . 25 And now, behold, I know that ye all, among whom I have gone
preaching the kingdom of God, shall see my face no more." (Acts 20:7, 25)*

"For I have not shunned to declare unto you all the counsel of God." (Acts 20:27)

*"And when they had preached the gospel to that city, and had taught many, they
returned again to Lystra, and to Iconium, and Antioch, 22 Confirming the souls of
the disciples, and exhorting them to continue in the faith, and that we must through
much tribulation enter into the kingdom of God." (Acts 14:21–22)*

2. CONNECTED TO ONE Brother

"And they continued stedfastly in the apostles' doctrine and fellowship, and in breaking of bread, and in prayers." (Acts 2:42)

"For as we have many members in one body, and all members have not the same office: 5 So we, being many, are one body in Christ, and every one members one of another." (Romans 12:4–5)

"And whether one member suffer, all the members suffer with it; or one member be honoured, all the members rejoice with it. 27 Now ye are the body of Christ, and members in particular." (1 Corinthians 12:26–27)

Through Spiritual RELATIONSHIPS

"A friend loveth at all times, and a brother is born for adversity." (Proverbs 17:17)

"Two are better than one; because they have a good reward for their labour. 10 For if they fall, the one will lift up his fellow: but woe to him that is alone when he falleth; for he hath not another to help him up." (Ecclesiastes 4:9–10)

LOVE ONE ANOTHER.

"A new commandment I give unto you, That ye love one another; as I have loved you, that ye also love one another." (John 13:34)

GREET, OR ACKNOWLEDGE, ONE ANOTHER.

"Greet one another with an holy kiss." (2 Corinthians 13:12)

SPEAK TRUTH TO ONE ANOTHER.

"Wherefore putting away lying, speak every man truth with his neighbour: for we are members one of another." (Ephesians 4:25)

BE KIND TO AND FORGIVING OF ONE ANOTHER.

"And be ye kind one to another, tenderhearted, forgiving one another, even as God for Christ's sake hath forgiven you." (Ephesians 4:32)

BEAR ONE ANOTHER'S BURDENS.

"Bear ye one another's burdens, and so fulfil the law of Christ." (Galatians 6:2)

COMFORT ONE ANOTHER.

"Wherefore comfort one another with these words." (1 Thessalonians 4:18)

"Wherefore comfort yourselves together, and edify one another, even as also ye do." (1 Thessalonians 5:11)

Through Spiritual Routines

"And they continued stedfastly in the apostles' doctrine and fellowship, and in breaking of bread, and in prayers." (Acts 2:42)

1. OBSERVING THE LORD'S TABLE

"And when he had given thanks, he brake it, and said, Take, eat: this is my body, which is broken for you: this do in remembrance of me. 25 After the same manner also he took the cup, when he had supped, saying, This cup is the new testament in my blood: this do ye, as oft as ye drink it, in remembrance of me. 26 For as often as ye eat this bread, and drink this cup, ye do shew the Lord's death till he come." (1 Corinthians 11:24–26)

2. CORPORATE PRAYER

"These all continued with one accord in prayer and supplication, with the women, and Mary the mother of Jesus, and with his brethren." (Acts 1:14)

"And when they had prayed, the place was shaken where they were assembled together; and they were all filled with the Holy Ghost, and they spake the word of God with boldness." (Acts 4:31)

"Whom they set before the apostles: and when they had prayed, they laid their hands on them." (Acts 6:6)

"Peter therefore was kept in prison: but prayer was made without ceasing of the church unto God for him." (Acts 12:5)

3. REGULAR ASSEMBLY

"And all that believed were together . . ." (Acts 2:44)

"And let us consider one another to provoke unto love and to good works: 25 Not forsaking the assembling of ourselves together, as the manner of some is; but exhorting one another: and so much the more, as ye see the day approaching." (Hebrews 10:24–25)

3. CONNECTED THROUGH SERVICE

"And all that believed were together, and had all things common; 45 And sold their possessions and goods, and parted them to all men, as every man had need. 46 And they, continuing daily with one accord in the temple, and breaking bread from house to house, did eat their meat with gladness and singleness of heart, 47 Praising God, and having favour with all the people. And the Lord added to the church daily such as should be saved. (Acts 2:44–47)

"And the multitude of them that believed were of one heart and of one soul: neither said any of them that ought of the things which he possessed was his own; but they had all things common." (Acts 4:32)

SERVE IN PRACTICAL WAYS.

"If I then, your Lord and Master, have washed your feet; ye also ought to wash one another's feet." (John 13:14)

GIVE TO THOSE IN NEED.

"I have shewed you all things, how that so labouring ye ought to support the weak, and to remember the words of the Lord Jesus, how he said, It is more blessed to give than to receive." (Acts 20:35)

SERVE THROUGH HOSPITALITY.

"Use hospitality one to another without grudging." (1 Peter 4:9)

USE THE SPIRITUAL GIFTS GOD HAS GIVEN YOU TO MINISTER TO THE BODY OF CHRIST.

"As every man hath received the gift, even so minister the same one to another, as good stewards of the manifold grace of God." (1 Peter 4:10)

"And whatsoever ye do, do it heartily, as to the Lord, and not unto men; 24 Knowing that of the Lord ye shall receive the reward of the inheritance: for ye serve the Lord Christ." (Colossians 3:23–24)

CONCLUSION

GROUP DISCUSSION

1. Was there anything from last week's devotionals or application exercises that was particularly meaningful or helpful to you? What passage of Scripture has been most reassuring to you this past week?

2. Some circumstances of grief literally isolate people from others. For example, one may be a full-time caretaker for someone who is bedridden, or one may have a disease that requires isolation because of a severely weak immune system. What strategies could an isolated Christian employ to address these sorts of challenges that make it difficult to stay connected during this season of grief?

3. What are some ways in which we can serve others? As you list ideas, you might add them under a few categories. For example, things we can do individually to encourage others, ways we can support one another emotionally, ways we can be a blessing to others as part of the church body, etc.

4. Has there been a time in your life when the prayers of other people for you have strengthened you in your time of need? If you feel comfortable doing so, share this story with the group.

5. What is one way the group can pray for you as it relates to grief this week? (A prayer request section is included at the end of this workbook so you can record the requests of other group members.)

SESSION NINE: DAY ONE

COME UNTO ME

Come unto me, all ye that labour and are heavy laden, and I will give you rest. (Matthew 11:28)

In January of 1982, Steven Callahan left the Canary Islands on a small sailing vessel he had designed and built himself. His plan was to sail to the island of Antigua in the Caribbean, crossing the Atlantic Ocean alone. One week into the trip his ship was struck and damaged. Callahan believed he had hit a whale, but the darkness made it impossible to be certain. He abandoned the sinking ship in a small life raft. But before the ship went down, he was able to salvage some critical survival gear, including a spear gun for fishing and solar distillers so he would have water to drink. But perhaps the most important thing he rescued was a copy of *Sea Survival: A Manual* which was written by another shipwreck survivor. It gave Callahan guidance and instruction he followed for the next seventy-six days until he finally reached land.

In times of grief and distress, Jesus gives us the things we need to find rest in Him. He does this in part by giving us three things to rest *upon*. He gives us His Word—specifically, the timeless truths of doctrine that serve as anchors for our soul during the stormy seasons of life. As Romans 15:4 tells us, "Whatsoever things were written aforetime were written for our learning, that we through patience and comfort of the Scriptures might have hope." When our strength is failing, we can lean on the rock of truth that will never fail.

Jesus also gives us His people, the church. In our fellow believers, we find the body of Christ, His hands and feet in this world, servants of His who are called to minister His love, grace, and mercy to one another (Romans 12; 1 Corinthians 12). And, like the fellow shipwreck survivor whose experience helped Steven Callahan survive his ordeal, we too find in our Christian brothers and sisters fellow travelers on the journey of faith, many of whom have walked the path of grief ahead of us. When we're not sure how to walk the road of grief, we do well to lean on the wisdom of those who have gone before us.

Finally, and most importantly, Jesus offers us one additional thing for us to rest upon during our season of grief: *Himself*. "Come unto me," He says, "and I will give you rest" (Matthew 11:28). We find rest in Jesus by intentionally sitting in His presence—through prayer, worship, and time spent in quiet, undistracted solitude with the One who loves us and gave His life for us.

TODAY'S TAKEAWAY

Grief can leave us feeling like we're shipwrecked, adrift at sea. But in God's Word, in His people, and in Jesus Himself, we have what we need to find our way to solid ground.

JOURNAL PROMPT

How has God given help to you through the testimonies, prayers, or companionship of other Christians?

SESSION NINE: DAY TWO

WHAT WE NEED

Do thy diligence to come shortly unto me . . . (2 Timothy 4:9)

As he sat in a cold, damp prison cell in Rome (2 Timothy 1:12, 16–17), Paul was lonely. He felt the sting of having been abandoned by those whom he had thought of as friends (2 Timothy 1:15; 4:10, 16). He had clearly reached the end of his earthly ministry, and he anticipated being executed in the near future: "I am now ready to be offered, and the time of my departure is at hand" (2 Timothy 4:6). Paul wrote these words to his protégé, Timothy, who, under Paul's tutelage, had become the pastor of the church at Ephesus. Unlike others, Timothy had proven to be a faithful friend—and so in his time of distress, Paul reached out to Timothy with some requests.

What did Paul ask for? He asked for three things specifically: two of his friends, a coat, and his books. "Do thy diligence to come shortly unto me: . . . Take Mark, and bring him with thee: . . . The cloke that I left at Troas with Carpus, when thou comest, bring with thee, and the books, but especially the parchments. . . . Do thy diligence to come before winter. . . ." (2 Timothy 4:9, 11, 13, 21).

These were simple needs, really. But they were real needs nonetheless. And Paul knew exactly where to go to find help: his brother in Christ.

We, too, have needs that can be met by our fellow wayfarers—our brothers and sisters in the Lord. What are those needs? The "one another" commands that we discussed in our lesson are suggestive of at least some of them:

- *Love* (John 13:34): When we are feeling weak and vulnerable, we need unconditional love and acceptance.
- *Acknowledgement* (2 Corinthians 13:12): During a season of grief, it's easy to feel forgotten. The simple act of greeting one another can be a real source of encouragement.

- *Truth* (Ephesians 4:25): When we are grieving, gentle reminders of the truths we know from Scripture can help us to stand "sure and stedfast" (Hebrews 6:19).
- *Kindness and forgiveness* (Ephesians 4:32): Grief can bring with it raw, sensitive emotions; in our own pain, we can sometimes be insensitive to the pain of others. We need the kindness and forgiveness of our brothers and sisters in Christ.
- *Burden-sharing* (Galatians 6:2): Whether it be a need for practical assistance, wise counsel, or other help, grief can overwhelm us with a slew of burdens. In the church, God has given us a team of burden-carriers.
- *Comfort* (1 Thessalonians 4:18; 5:11): The "God of all comfort" uses His people to minister His comfort to us during our times of sorrow (2 Corinthians 1:3–5).

As we face the journey of grief ahead of us, we are not alone. God has placed what we need for this moment, for this time and place, within reach. Literally within reach—a piece of paper to write a letter, a cell phone to send a text, a computer to write an email, or a telephone to place a call. Let's give ourselves permission, like Paul, to reach out for what we need.

TODAY'S TAKEAWAY

Our Lord has given us His people to be our traveling companions; they have much of what we need for the journey.

JOURNAL PROMPT

Which of the needs from the above list are you feeling most acutely right now? Share those needs with the Lord and ask Him to show you who you might be able to reach out to for what you need.

SESSION NINE: DAY THREE

WITH THESE WORDS

Wherefore comfort one another with these words.(1 Thessalonians 4:18)

Mary Lincoln, also known as "Mamie" was the granddaughter of one of America's most famous presidents. She lived in New York City until her death in 1938. When she died, an unknown treasure was discovered and turned over to the Library of Congress—Mary Lincoln had a small box that held the contents of Abraham Lincoln's pockets on the night he was assassinated. One of the things he was carrying that night in Ford's Theatre was a letter to the editor of a Washington newspaper praising Lincoln for his singleness of purpose. In the face of constant attack and criticism, Lincoln greatly valued words of praise and encouragement.

The world is filled with people who are quick to critique and condemn. Often we feel alone and isolated, wishing that someone would see our grief and care enough to say a kind word. The absence of such encouragement makes it much more difficult to keep going. Even Jesus benefited from this principle. When Satan tempted Jesus, Jesus overcame each attack with the words of Scripture. Yet, when the temptation was over, Jesus was alone."*Then the devil leaveth him, and, behold, angels came and ministered unto him*" (Matthew 4:11).

We have a great opportunity to strengthen the body of Christ simply by sharing words of hope and encouragement with each other. Paul wrote, "*Wherefore comfort one another with these words*" (1 Thessalonians 4:18).

The very Word of God brings comfort to our hearts. Sometimes Christians hesitate to comfort one another with Scripture because they don't want to come off as rattling off pat answers to deep pain. And some Christians do, at times, use the Word of God in a way that feels insensitive or inappropriate to the moment.

But the fact remains that Scripture is a key component in the Christian's tool kit—arguably, in fact, the *primary* tool we are given with which to comfort one another. The Word of God, properly applied to our hearts, can bring strength, healing, and comfort that we didn't imagine possible.

The Holy Spirit can and will use the truth of His Word to speak comfort to our souls—even in cases when the human messenger is less than ideal in his or her delivery of the message.

Knowing that the promises of Scripture provide comfort in grief should lead us to two questions:

1. In what ways am I receiving the words of Scripture as comfort from other believers? (Are you listening to preaching and teaching in your church? Are you allowing friends to speak into your life reminding you of God's promises and the help from His Word?)
2. In what ways am I sharing the comfort of God's Word with others?

TODAY'S TAKEAWAY

The very words of God are the richest, deepest, most healing source of comfort there is to be found.

JOURNAL PROMPT

What are your answers to the two questions presented at the end of today's devotion? Is there anything you want or need to change based on those answers?

SESSION NINE: DAY FOUR

THE POWER OF HABIT

Teaching us that, denying ungodliness and worldly lusts, we should live soberly, righteously, and godly, in this present world . . . (Titus 2:12)

In times of grief, our deeply engrained habits can be both our friend and our enemy. Good habits can keep us moving forward even when we're tired physically, emotionally, or spiritually. Bad habits can keep us stuck, distract us, or pull us downward into destructive patterns of behavior. In the face of this, we may find ourselves wanting to build (or maintain) good habits and find ways to break bad ones. But what, exactly, are habits—and how can they be changed?

In *Atomic Habits: An Easy & Proven Way to Build Good Habits & Break Bad Ones*, author James Clear defines a habit as "a routine or behavior that is performed regularly—and, in many cases, automatically." [1] Habits, both good and bad, are formed through repetition; the more they are repeated, the more "automatic" they become. [2] (Think, for example, of the process you went through to learn how to ride a bike or drive a car.) Lasting *change* in one's habits, in turn, comes about through a process of small, incremental steps that have a cumulative effect over time. As Clear explains it, making just a one percent change per day in the direction you want to go "compounds" over time.[3]

The relevance of these ideas about habit formation and change to our spiritual lives, particularly during a season of grief, is significant. Remaining faithful to spiritual routines such as gathering together with other believers regularly for worship and teaching, daily spending time in prayer, and observing the Lord's Table with our church family, can help keep us "on track" when our emotions are weighed down with grief, or even feeling dead or unruly. This isn't about a slavish, legalistic attempt to "check the boxes." Rather, these practices help us to keep moving forward even when our emotions aren't cooperating.

You see, emotions tend to follow action. Start acting kindly toward someone you don't like, and you're likely to start feeling more favorably toward them over time. Choose to exhibit patience toward a coworker on a regular basis, and your feelings of irritation and impatience will likely diminish.

Similarly, when we are struggling with grief, we may not *feel* like spending time in fellowship with other believers, engaging in corporate prayer, or participating in the observance of the Lord's Table. We may feel too tired and weary to engage in conversation with others or the Lord; we may even feel unworthy or unwelcome in their presence. But as we engage consistently in these spiritual routines, we are likely to find our hearts warming up once again—perhaps not immediately, but eventually.

Titus 2:11–12 tells us that "the grace of God that bringeth salvation hath appeared to all men, Teaching us that, denying ungodliness and worldly lusts, we should live soberly, righteously, and godly, in this present world." The practical reality is that this way of living does not happen automatically. It is the result of daily choices, of small, incremental steps in the right direction. And a great many of these choices are made at the level of habit. Understanding—and harnessing—the power of habits and routines is, therefore, one key to making progress in our spiritual lives both now, during our present season of grief, and in the days and years ahead.

TODAY'S TAKEAWAY

Our personal habits and spiritual routines can help to keep us moving forward in living "soberly, righteously, and godly" (Titus 2:12) even when we are physically, emotionally, or spiritually tired.

JOURNAL PROMPT

What good habits in your life are creating peace, comfort, or a sense of "normalcy" during this season of grief? What needed habit do you want to develop to help you move forward?

SESSION NINE: DAY FIVE

SERVING AS TO THE LORD

And whatsoever ye do, do it heartily, as to the Lord, and not unto men; Knowing that of the Lord ye shall receive the reward of the inheritance: for ye serve the Lord Christ. (Colossians 3:23–24)

Whether through tangible acts of service, financial giving, exercising hospitality, or using our spiritual gifts to help the body of Christ, every Christian needs to be involved in serving others. But serving others while we are grieving can be difficult. Our natural instincts are to withdraw— to hibernate in a cave while our wounds heal. Even the thought of "serving" can seem overwhelming at a time like this. *How can I possibly add one more thing onto the plate when I'm dealing with so much already?*

But service is actually good for us. It helps keep us connected with the body of Christ, and it is in that connection that healing is found.

In the face of these realities, it's helpful to remember several things about service:

When it comes to service, it's about quality, not quantity. Faithful service need not be a matter of doing large-scale, time- or energy-consuming activities. For you, serving faithfully during this season may simply mean reaching out to one person this week with a word of encouragement or a thoughtful card. What matters isn't how *much* you're doing as much as the fact *that you're doing it. Are you doing something* to share God's love—the very love upon which you're depending—during this time?

We serve others by allowing them to serve us. As the body of Christ, we are called to "bear . . . one another's burdens, and so fulfil the law of Christ" (Galatians 6:2). In bearing each other's burdens, we follow in the footsteps of our Savior, who willingly bore our burdens—especially the burden of our sin—on His shoulders (Isaiah 53:4–6).

Sometimes we're called to bear the burdens of others; at other times, we are the ones who need others to help us shoulder the load. It can be hard to find ourselves in that position—we naturally prefer to be the "strong" ones, the ones who (seemingly) "have it all together." But the reality is that the opportunity to share one another's burdens is actually a *gift*—one of the greatest gifts that our Lord gives to His children. When we allow others to bear our burdens with us, we grant them the opportunity to experience that gift. Let us not deprive others—or *ourselves*—of the gift of sharing our burdens with one another.

When we serve, we are actually serving our Savior. For some of us, the challenge of serving during a time of grief is that we can't *escape* the need to serve. For example, we may be the primary caregiver for an ailing spouse, an elderly parent, a child with disabilities, or someone else with intense, ongoing healthcare or other needs. For those of us in this situation, we need to remember that such caregiving can *itself* be a form of service to the Lord when it is done from the heart for Him.

When done "as to the Lord" (Colossians 3:23), our service becomes a pleasing offering of love and worship that is received as service given directly to Christ Himself: "And the King shall answer and say unto them, Verily I say unto you, Inasmuch as ye have done it unto one of the least of these my brethren, ye have done it unto me" (Matthew 25:40).

TODAY'S TAKEAWAY

Whatever your service looks like during this season of grief, do it "heartily, as to the Lord" (Colossians 3:23), and it will be pleasing to Him.

JOURNAL PROMPT

Ask the Lord to reveal to you what you have to give to others even in the midst of your weariness.

PERSONAL APPLICATION

The following exercises are intended to give you an opportunity to apply the things you're learning and discussing in the group meetings and daily devotionals. They don't have to be done in any particular sequence or on a particular day of the week. If you only have the physical or emotional energy to complete one of these exercises, that's fine. The point is to allow the Spirit of God to minister to your heart during this time of grief.

STAYING CONNECTED THROUGH SPIRITUAL RELATIONSHIPS

Throughout the New Testament, God gives many instructions for the type of relationships that Christians should share with each other in the local church. Sometimes these are referred to as the "one another" commands because the verses include the phrase "one another."

In our lesson we looked at a few of these commands:

- Love one another (John 13:34).
- Greet, or acknowledge, one another (2 Corinthians 13:12).
- Speak truth to one another (Ephesians 4:25).
- Be kind to and forgiving of one another (Ephesians 4:32).
- Bear one another's burdens (Galatians 6:2).
- Comfort one another (1 Thessalonians 4:18; 5:11).

We saw in our Day 2 devotional for this week that each of these commands reflects a genuine need that we all share—to be loved, acknowledged, forgiven, and so forth. At the end of that devotional, you were encouraged to ask the Lord to show you who you might turn to for help in meeting any of these needs that you're feeling especially strongly right now.

Here, we're going to "flip the script" a bit. The question now becomes, who might the Lord be asking *you* to serve in one of these ways?

- O **Action Item:** As you consider the "one another" commands, which one(s) does your heart resonate with? Choose one of these and then reach out to someone else in your church community, intentionally blessing them by living out that command in their life. In doing so, you'll find that you can still be used by God to minister to those around you, even as you go through your own season of grief.

____

____

____

____

HARNESSING THE POWER OF HABITS AND ROUTINES

In our devotional for Day 4 of this week, we considered the power (for better and for worse) that our habits and routines have in our lives during seasons of grief. Here, we're going to explore in greater detail what it looks like to go about *changing* our habit structure.

In his book *Atomic Habits*, James Clear discusses what he calls the "Four Laws of Behavior Change." If you want to start (or improve) a good habit,

1. "Make it Obvious." For example, if you want to make sure you drink more water each day, place water bottles throughout your home or workplace.

2. “Make it Attractive.” One way to do this is to “pair an action you want to do with an action you need to do.”

3. “Make it Easy.” For example, “Create an environment where doing the right thing is as easy as possible.”

4. “Make it Satisfying.” When working to build a good habit, ensure that every performance of that new action receives some kind of immediate reward, however small it may be.

○ **Action item:** After reviewing your response to the journal prompt at the end of the Day 4 devotional, identify one or two of the *good* habits in your life that have continued despite your current challenging circumstances. Take a moment to thank the Lord for the way His Holy Spirit is using those routines in your life to help you keep moving forward through grief.

Now, identify one or two habits that you would like to see *developed* in your life during this season of grief. For each of these, see if you can come up with a specific way to make that habit “Obvious,” “Attractive,” “Easy,” and/or “Satisfying.” Begin implementing these strategies in the days ahead in small, easily achievable steps.

STABILIZING YOUR SOUL

The final meal that Jesus had before He was betrayed was shared with His disciples. For the disciples, this would have been a special time of connection with their Lord—though one tinged with anticipatory grief. They were confused. They knew things weren't going well, but they didn't understand what was going on or what was about to happen. In that special time Jesus offered them words of comfort and encouragement that they would never forget: "... I go to prepare a place for you. And if I go and prepare a place for you, I will come again, and receive you unto myself; that where I am, there ye may be also" (John 14:2–3). Knowing that His disciples were about to go through a time of unimaginable grief, Jesus shared His heart with them: He loved them and would be with them.

Jesus loves you, too. And He is with you now.

- ○ **Action item:** Plan a time to sit in Jesus' presence this week as you consider His promise to be with you. You might prepare a picnic in a park or go to your favorite hiking spot. Wherever you go and whatever you do, allow the Lord's presence to bring you comfort and encouragement as you continue to move forward through this season of your life.

AND THE PEACE OF GOD, WHICH PASSETH ALL UNDERSTANDING, SHALL KEEP YOUR HEARTS AND MINDS THROUGH CHRIST JESUS. (PHILIPPIANS 4:7)

EXPERIENCING GOD'S PEACE

WHEN I AM STRESSED

Session Notes

Discussion

Devotional Readings

1. Giving Thanks in All Things
2. The Lord is Near
3. Just in Time
4. Peace in His Presence
5. Think on These Things

Personal Application

EXPERIENCING GOD'S PEACE

"Be careful for nothing; but in every thing by prayer and supplication with thanksgiving let your requests be made known unto God. 7 And the peace of God, which passeth all understanding, shall keep your hearts and minds through Christ Jesus. 8 Finally, brethren, whatsoever things are true, whatsoever things are honest, whatsoever things are just, whatsoever things are pure, whatsoever things are lovely, whatsoever things are of good report; if there be any virtue, and if there be any praise, think on these things." (Philippians 4:6–8)

INTRODUCTION

____

____

____

"Rejoice in the Lord alway: and again I say, Rejoice. 5 Let your moderation be known unto all men. The Lord is at hand. 6 Be careful for nothing; but in every thing by prayer and supplication with thanksgiving let your requests be made known unto God. 7 And the peace of God, which passeth all understanding, shall keep your hearts and minds through Christ Jesus. 8 Finally, brethren, whatsoever things are true, whatsoever things are honest, whatsoever things are just, whatsoever things are pure, whatsoever things are lovely, whatsoever things are of good report; if there be any virtue, and if there be any praise, think on these things." (Philippians 4:4–8)

"And be not conformed to this world: but be ye transformed by the renewing of your mind, that ye may prove what is that good, and acceptable, and perfect, will of God." (Romans 12:2)

1. PRAISE: REJOICE IN THE LORD

"Rejoice in the Lord alway: and again I say, Rejoice." (Philippians 4:4)

The DICISION of Praise

"Although the fig tree shall not blossom, neither shall fruit be in the vines; the labour of the olive shall fail, and the fields shall yield no meat; the flock shall be cut

off from the fold, and there shall be no herd in the stalls: 18 Yet I will rejoice in the LORD, I will joy in the God of my salvation." (Habakkuk 3:17–18)

The OBJECT of Praise

"He is thy praise, and he is thy God, that hath done for thee these great and terrible things, which thine eyes have seen." (Deuteronomy 10:21)

"And they departed from the presence of the council, rejoicing that they were counted worthy to suffer shame for his name." (Acts 5:41)

FOUR PRACTICAL WAYS TO PRAISE THE LORD IN MOMENTS OF STRESS

1. ***Sing.***

   "I will be glad and rejoice in thee: I will sing praise to thy name, O thou most High." (Psalm 9:2)

2. ***Read Psalms.***

   "Praise ye the LORD. O give thanks unto the LORD; for he is good: for his mercy endureth for ever." (Psalm 106:1)

3. ***Consider His attributes.***

   "Rejoice in the LORD, ye righteous; and give thanks at the remembrance of his holiness." (Psalm 97:12)

4. ***Remember His works.***

   "I will remember the works of the LORD: surely I will remember thy wonders of old. I will meditate also of all thy work, and talk of thy doings." (Psalm 77:11-12)

2. POISE: REMEMBER THE LORD'S NEARNESS

"Let your moderation be known unto all men. The Lord is at hand." (Philippians 4:5)

Definition: *Moderation,* from *epieikes:* "suitable, equitable, fair, sweet reasonableness.

"Let your conversation be without covetousness; and be content with such things as ye have: for he hath said, I will never leave thee, nor forsake thee. 6 So that we may boldly say, The Lord is my helper, and I will not fear what man shall do unto me." (Hebrews 13:5–6)

"Be ye also patient; stablish your hearts: for the coming of the Lord draweth nigh." (James 5:8)

"These things I have spoken unto you, that in me ye might have peace. In the world ye shall have tribulation: but be of good cheer; I have overcome the world." (John 16:33)

"God is our refuge and strength, a very present help in trouble.... 10 Be still, and know that I am God..." (Psalm 46:1, 10)

"Now it came to pass, as they went, that he entered into a certain village: and a certain woman named Martha received him into her house. 39 And she had a sister called Mary, which also sat at Jesus' feet, and heard his word. 40 But Martha was cumbered about much serving, and came to him, and said, Lord, dost thou not care that my sister hath left me to serve alone? bid her therefore that she help me. 41 And Jesus answered and said unto her, Martha, Martha, thou art careful and troubled about many things: 42 But one thing is needful: and Mary hath chosen that good part, which shall not be taken away from her." (Luke 10:38–42)

3. PRAYER: REQUEST HELP FROM THE LORD

"Be careful for nothing; but in every thing by prayer and supplication with thanksgiving let your requests be made known unto God." (Philippians 4:6)

Request without WORRY

Quote: *"High adrenaline, caused by overextension and stress, depletes the brain's natural tranquilizers and sets the stage for high anxiety."*—**Dr. Archibald Hart**

Quote: *"Turn every care into a prayer."*—**John Haggai**

Request with THANKSGIVING

Quote: *"Gratitude never comes from avoiding difficulty, but from finding yourself sustained through it."*—**Randy Alcorn**

"In every thing give thanks: for this is the will of God in Christ Jesus concerning you." (1 Thessalonians 5:18)

4. PEACE: REST IN THE LORD

"And the peace of God, which passeth all understanding, shall keep your hearts and minds through Christ Jesus." (Philippians 4:7)

"Therefore being justified by faith, we have peace with God through our Lord Jesus Christ: 2 By whom also we have access by faith into this grace wherein we stand, and rejoice in hope of the glory of God." (Romans 5:1–2)

"Thou wilt keep him in perfect peace, whose mind is stayed on thee: because he trusteth in thee. 4 Trust ye in the LORD for ever: for in the LORD JEHOVAH is everlasting strength:" (Isaiah 26:3–4)

5. PURITY: REFLECT ON WHAT IS PLEASING TO THE LORD

"Finally, brethren, whatsoever things are true, whatsoever things are honest, whatsoever things are just, whatsoever things are pure, whatsoever things are lovely, whatsoever things are of good report; if there be any virtue, and if there be any praise, think on these things." (Philippians 4:8)

The DISCRIPTION of Pure Thoughts

- **True** (Greek: *alethes*)—loving the truth, speaking the truth; true in character
- **Honest** (Greek: *semnos*)—to be venerated for character, honorable
- **Just** (Greek: *dikaios*)—righteous, upright, approved of God
- **Pure** (Greek: *hagnos*)—free from carnality, chaste, modest, clean
- **Lovely** (Greek: *prosphiles*)—acceptable, pleasing, winsome, amiable
- **Of good report** (Greek: *euphemos*)—sounding well; highly regarded, well thought of

The DEVELOPMENT of Pure Thoughts

"Casting down imaginations, and every high thing that exalteth itself against the knowledge of God, and bringing into captivity every thought to the obedience of Christ;" (2 Corinthians 10:5)

CONCLUSION

GROUP DISCUSSION

1. Was there anything from last week's devotionals or application exercises that was particularly meaningful or helpful to you? What passage of Scripture has been most reassuring to you this past week?

2. What are some of the reasons for stress you have noticed that are unique to grief?

3. One of the challenges of stress is that sometimes we don't recognize it until it has overtaken our minds. What are some of the early signs of stress that might prompt us to seek God's help?

4. What are some practical ways in which we can help ourselves remember the Lord's nearness when we are feeling stressed?

5. What is one way the group can pray for you as it relates to grief this week? (A prayer request section is included at the end of this workbook so you can record the requests of other group members.)

SESSION TEN: DAY ONE

GIVING THANKS IN ALL THINGS

In every thing give thanks: for this is the will of God in Christ Jesus concerning you. (1 Thessalonians 5:18)

On February 28, 1944, Corrie ten Boom's family house in the Dutch town of Haarlem was raided by the Nazis.[1] The ten Boom family had been collaborating with the Dutch Resistance and had been harboring Jews and other fugitives from the Nazis. On days when the Nazis conducted security sweeps of their neighborhood, the refugees who were currently in the ten Boom home would pile into a secret hiding place—a small compartment behind a false wall in Corrie's bedroom—until it was safe to reemerge. On this day, however, a fellow Dutch citizen had reported the ten Booms to the Nazis, and their own lives were about to change forever.

The Nazis failed to discover the six fugitives who were hiding behind Corrie's bedroom wall, but they did arrest some thirty or so others who were in and around the house that day, including the entire ten Boom family. Corrie, her older sister Betsie, and their father Casper were sent to Scheveningen Prison, where Casper died ten days later. Corrie and Betsie were eventually transferred to Ravensbrück, a labor camp for women that was notorious for its harsh conditions.

At Ravensbrück, the ten Boom sisters witnessed and experienced unimaginable horrors, but they also saw God work in powerful, even miraculous, ways. Corrie had been able to smuggle a Bible into the camp with her, and with that precious book Corrie and Betsie reached out to their fellow inmates with the love of God and the hope of the gospel. Night after night, they held clandestine worship "services" in their barracks, reading the words of Scripture aloud as their fellow prisoners translated their words into other languages. Oddly, their ever-vigilant guards never interfered with these services, nor even set foot in their barracks.

Among other degradations the ten Booms experienced at Ravensbrück, they had to endure the torment of being bitten incessantly by the fleas that populated the barracks in which they were housed. But even then,

Corrie's sister Betsie had a special gift for seeing God's hand at work. Citing 1 Thessalonians 5:18, Betsie urged Corrie to give thanks for the fleas: "Give thanks in *all* circumstances," Betsie said. "It doesn't say, 'in pleasant circumstances.' Fleas are part of this place where God has put us." And so, despite Corrie's skepticism, the ten Boom sisters "stood between piers of bunks and gave thanks for fleas."[2]

Betsie would later discover that it was precisely *because* of the fleas that the Nazi guards refused to enter Barracks 28. In God's providence, He had used the presence of tiny, unpleasant, parasitic insects to work His purposes in the darkest of places. And as a result, many of the prisoners at Ravensbrück came to faith in Christ.

First Thessalonians 5:18 does not require us to *enjoy* or find pleasure in the things that are happening to us. Whether it be the discomfort of flea bites or the grief of losing a loved one, there are many things in life that cause pain and suffering. And we can acknowledge those things as such. But what this verse *does* do is invite us to look for God's hand at work all around us. And when we learn to recognize His work in our lives, we will find ourselves with every reason to give thanks.

TODAY'S TAKEAWAY

It is God's will that we express thanksgiving regardless of our circumstances because that exercises our faith in God and creates opportunity for us to experience His faithfulness.

JOURNAL PROMPT

Betsie gave thanks for the fleas before she knew they were a tool of protection for Barracks 28. Are there metaphorical "fleas" in your life? Journal your list of "fleas" and ask the Lord to begin revealing to you how He can use these circumstances for your good.

SESSION TEN: DAY TWO

THE LORD IS NEAR

Let your moderation be known unto all men. The Lord is at hand. (Philippians 4:5)

It had been a long day. Jesus had spent most of it standing in a boat, teaching about the kingdom of God to the crowds of people who had gathered on the shoreline (Mark 4:1–34). Now, Jesus was tired. So, he told His disciples to cast off and head for the other side of the lake, while He retired to the back of the boat to take a nap.

Sometime during the journey, a furious storm arose. The ship was taking on water. But Jesus continued to sleep. Fearing for their lives, the disciples woke Jesus up and asked Him frantically, "Master, carest thou not that we perish?"

In response, Jesus simply stood up, "rebuked the wind, and said unto the sea, Peace, be still. And the wind ceased, and there was a great calm" (Mark 4:39).

Turning to His disciples, He asked them, "Why are ye so fearful? how is it that ye have no faith?" (Mark 4:40).

Often what we notice when we read this story in Mark 4 is the power of God to miraculously calm the storm—simply by speaking to the wind and waves. But consider for a moment another remarkable aspect of this incident—the peacefulness of Jesus in the midst of a storm. Jesus *slept* while the storm raged. And then when He awoke, He didn't fret or worry. He simply *spoke* to the storm.

What made the difference between Jesus' response to the storm and that of His frightened disciples? The difference was that He knew who He was; they had not yet grasped that reality. He had a calm poise that they lacked because they didn't understand the significance of His presence with them.

Because Jesus was with them, they were—and always had been—safe, no matter how strong the storm blew and no matter how much water their ship took on. Jesus was always in control of that situation, and they had nothing to fear.

The questions Jesus asked His disciples are worth asking ourselves: "Why are ye so fearful? how is it that ye have no faith?" Have we really grasped—appreciated—the reality of who it is that walks with us through this dark, fearful storm of grief in which we now find ourselves?

When we are stressed, we tend to overreact to situations. Our frayed nerves respond out of proportion to the circumstances we face. But Philippians 4:5 gives us an amazing truth to counter our anxious thoughts: "Let your moderation be known unto all men. The Lord is at hand." In effect, Philippians 4:5 is telling us to measure out our responses to stressful situations in proportion to the realities of those circumstances—most importantly, the fact that "the Lord is at hand." If we really believe that the Lord is with us, it should impact how we respond to the stressful and difficult circumstances in our lives.

How do we achieve this sort of *moderation*? We do so by reflecting on the truth of what Scripture has revealed: our Lord is with us now and until the end of time (Hebrews 13:5–6; Matthew 28:20), and He is coming again some day to bring us to glory (James 5:8).

TODAY'S TAKEAWAY

When we remember the Lord's nearness—His presence with us and His soon return—it settles our souls and produces a poise that reflects a heart at rest in God.

JOURNAL PROMPT

What are some recurring situations in which you tend to overreact to other people or circumstances? How can remembering that "the Lord is at hand" (Philippians 4:5) help give you added perspective in these moments?

SESSION TEN: DAY THREE

JUST IN TIME

Pray without ceasing. (1 Thessalonians 5:17)

George Müller (1805–1898) was a Christian pastor and evangelist who cared for the many orphans on the street. In 1849 he founded the Ashley Down orphanage in the English town of Bristol to serve some three hundred orphans. By 1870, over 1,700 children were being served at a time. All told, it's estimated that over the course of his lifetime, Müller cared for more than 10,000 orphans.

Müller was a fastidious record keeper. Even the smallest donation—whether of money, material goods, or services—that was extended to the orphanage received an acknowledgment and receipt from Mr. Müller. He was also a prayer warrior. He prayed for everything, and he prayed with expectation: whatever was needed, he was confident the Lord would provide. Accordingly, he accepted only unsolicited gifts, and he refused to go into debt to build the orphanage or to keep its doors open, even when finances were tight—as they frequently were. He was a man of faith and a man of prayer.

This faith was tested many times. On one famous occasion, the orphanage was completely out of food, but Müller brought the children to the breakfast table and gave thanks as if the food were already there. As Müller concluded his prayer, a baker knocked on the front door with enough fresh bread for all the residents. Shortly after this, there was another knock on the door: a milk man offered them fresh milk because his wagon had broken down right in front of the orphanage. Before long, everything needed to feed the children that morning was on hand. Once again, the Lord had provided exactly what was needed.

Of course, it is not that the Lord *needed* Müller's prayers before He could provide for the children at the orphanage—God's ability to provide is not dependent upon our actions, including prayer. Instead, God invites us to "let [our] requests be made known" to Him (Philippians 4:6) so that *we* can experience the joy of seeing His provision in response to our prayers, and so our faith will be strengthened.

Importantly, though, when it comes to providing for our needs, our Lord is always "just in time." He doesn't arrive too early, nor does He arrive too late. It may feel to us like He is delaying unnecessarily or even ignoring our pleas for help. But throughout the pages of Scripture, we see a God who knows exactly what His children need and who delights in taking good care of them. And throughout the pages of human history, we hear the testimonies of His people who have experienced His sustaining care in a myriad of ways—sometimes miraculously, other times through the ordinary events of everyday life.

"Pray without ceasing," we are instructed in 1 Thessalonians 5:17. Pray in good times and in bad. Pray in seasons of happiness and in time of grief. Pray for the "big" things in life and for the "little" things. And pray with expectation. When we do, we can rest assured that the same God who could provide a meal for hungry orphans in an English town in the 1800s can also provide for us during our times of grief today.

TODAY'S TAKEAWAY

When we lay our requests before our Heavenly Father and wait upon Him expectantly, our faith is strengthened as we witness the overflowing abundance of His gracious and ever-present provision in our lives—provision that always arrives at just the right time.

JOURNAL PROMPT

All of us are tempted to worry when we should pray. What are some current needs in your life over which you are tempted to worry? How can you use those feelings of worry as a prompt to pray?

SESSION TEN: DAY FOUR

PEACE IN HIS PRESENCE

And the peace of God, which passeth all understanding, shall keep your hearts and minds through Christ Jesus. (Philippians 4:7)

Many a parent has awakened during the night to the frightened cries of a young child who has had a nightmare. In those moments, what that child needs most is to know that he is safe. The loving presence of his mommy or daddy at his bedside calms his mind and soothes his heart, enabling him to rest once again.

Grief can leave us feeling not only stressed, but also scared and vulnerable. Unanswered (and perhaps unanswerable) questions about the future can seem overwhelming. Fear-filled thoughts can make it difficult to breathe. Old habits that we thought had been conquered long ago can rear their tempting heads once again. Sometimes, it can feel like we're literally under attack—whether from the enemy or just from our own weaknesses.

In such times, we need a place of refuge to which we can run. The Lord Himself is that place. His presence is where we can find the peace we need when we feel like we're under attack.

We saw in our lesson that we have peace *with* God (Romans 5:1–2) and we have the peace *of* God (Isaiah 26:3–4). We also have the *protection* of God's peace. As Philippians 4:7 assures us, God's peace protects our hearts and minds. It guards us from the disastrous effects of anxiety or stress-filled responses to our circumstances.

In much the same way as a nation or a city cannot be overrun or conquered when it is well-defended, God's peace protects us from being defeated by the spiritual attacks that the enemy launches against us and helps us regain our footing when our frailties and weaknesses cause us to stumble. When we rest in the Lord's protection, He becomes our "strong tower" (Proverbs 18:10; Psalm 61:3)—the one to whom we can run and be safe.

“I am with you always, even unto the end of the world,” Jesus told His disciples before He returned to Heaven (Matthew 28:20). And He says this same thing to us today. He is with us in the midst of our pain and sorrow. He knows the grief we feel, and He stands with us in it. Not only that, but He holds our hand as we walk along the sometimes treacherous path of life. With the Lord by our side, we can walk securely and with confidence even as we grieve.

TODAY'S TAKEAWAY

For God's children, peace is not found in the absence of trouble, but in the very presence of Christ Himself.

JOURNAL PROMPT

In what ways has the Lord made his presence known to you recently? Take some time to thank Him for being a “strong tower” to which you can run for refuge.

SESSION TEN: DAY FIVE

THINK ON THESE THINGS

Finally, brethren, whatsoever things are true, whatsoever things are honest, whatsoever things are just, whatsoever things are pure, whatsoever things are lovely, whatsoever things are of good report; if there be any virtue, and if there be any praise, think on these things. (Philippians 4:8)

As we've discussed previously, during a season of grief our thoughts, if left unchecked, can quickly lead us into dangerous and self-destructive territory. It is in times like these that it's especially important to bring "into captivity every thought to the obedience of Christ," as 2 Corinthians 10:5 instructs us. The good news is that our thoughts *can* be taken "captive" to Christ—but it requires an intentional choice on our part.

It's striking how often Scripture speaks of the importance of the life of the mind. On the one hand, sin begins in the mind (Matthew 5:28). On the other hand, transformation begins with the "renewing" of our minds, as Romans 12:2 tells us. And the result of transformation is discernment: "that ye may prove what is that good, and acceptable, and perfect, will of God" (Romans 12:2).

But how do we do this? How do we go about "renewing" our minds? Here, Philippians 4:8 is instructive: "Finally, brethren, whatsoever things are true, whatsoever things are honest, whatsoever things are just, whatsoever things are pure, whatsoever things are lovely, whatsoever things are of good report; if there be any virtue, and if there be any praise, think on these things." As we saw in our group session, to *think on* something is to concentrate our focus on it. It is to make a deliberate choice to consider it, to meditate on it. Accordingly, anytime the Holy Spirit convicts us that our thinking does not line up with what is true, honest, just, pure, lovely, and of good report, we need to pause and purposefully refocus our thoughts.

"Blessed are the pure in heart: for they shall see God," Jesus said in His famous Sermon on the Mount (Matthew 5:8). Purity of the heart is deeply connected with purity of the mind. When our minds are pure—focused on things that are true, honest, just, pure, lovely and of good report

(Philippians 4:8)—we are able to see more clearly God's hand at work in our lives and in the world around us. And when we can see that, we're less likely to incline our hearts toward the things that will lead us astray—false "gods" that offer us promises of security but in the end will lead only to chaos and destruction.

How desperately we need this kind of purity—of heart and mind—during our season of grief! Let us reach out to the one who can wash us and make us "whiter than snow" (Psalm 51:7).

TODAY'S TAKEAWAY

When your thoughts start to take you in dangerous, self-destructive, or unhealthy directions, choose to take them captive to Christ (2 Corinthians 10:5) by intentionally focusing on things that are true, honest, just, pure, lovely and "of good report" (Philippians 4:8).

JOURNAL PROMPT

Are there any thoughts that you find yourself struggling with repeatedly that threaten to lead you in dangerous, self-destructive, or unhealthy directions? If so, identify them here and ask the Holy Spirit to speak His truth into your heart about each of these matters.

PERSONAL APPLICATION

The following exercises are intended to give you an opportunity to apply the things you're learning and discussing in the group meetings and daily devotionals. They don't have to be done in any particular sequence or on a particular day of the week. If you only have the physical or emotional energy to complete one of these exercises, that's fine. The point is to allow the Spirit of God to minister to your heart during this time of grief.

PRAISING THE LORD IN MOMENTS OF STRESS

We saw in our group session that one of the best ways we can respond to stressful situations is to intentionally choose to praise God and rejoice in Him. And we saw four practical ways to praise the Lord in these moments of stress:

1. *Sing* (Psalm 9:2). Songs of praise give us both the words and the voice to exercise our choice to praise God. We can sing about His greatness and His attributes even as the tears fall. And often, the very process of singing releases some of our stress.

2. *Read* Psalms (Psalm 106:1). Throughout the Psalms, we see the psalmists making choices of praise, even in moments of trial and grief. These psalms focus on the unchanging attributes of God. As we read them—and even use their words in prayer to the Lord—they help us to praise Him.

3. *Consider God's attributes* (Psalm 97:12). This is the heart of what it means to rejoice in the Lord. It is to rejoice in who He is. He is good, righteous, just, faithful, true, holy, and so much more.

4. *Remember the Lord's works* (Psalm 77:11–12). Consider what God has done for you in the past. Remembering His goodness and faithfulness in the past will build your trust in Him in the present.

○ **Action Item:** For each of these practical means of praising God, take a few moments to brainstorm specific ways you might be able to put them into practice when you're feeling stressed. Some suggestive prompts are included here.

1. Sing.
   Three of my favorite songs of praise are . . .

   ____

   ____

2. Read Psalms.
   Three Psalms that extol God's greatness are . . .

   ____

   ____

3. Consider God's attributes.
   God's praiseworthy attributes include (list as many as you can think of) . . .

   ____

   ____

4. Remember the Lord's works.
   Three times I remember God's goodness and faithfulness at work in my life are . . .

   ____

   ____

Now, keep this list handy, and use one of these methods of praising God next time you're feeling stressed.

TAKING EVERY THOUGHT CAPTIVE

Second Corinthians 10:5 instructs us to cast out wrong thoughts and bring our thoughts into captivity to, or into the control of, obedience to Christ.

One of the practical ways to do this is to avoid extended time with people, programs, media feeds, books, or any other sources that are negative or frivolous. In seasons of grief, we probably have enough negativity coming at us to not need to also fill our minds with hours a day of news or negative websites or social media streams.

O **Action item:** Identify any source of negative "input" that needs to be eliminated from your life.

On the positive side, a practical way to think on what is true, honest, just, pure, lovely, and of good report is to fill our minds and our hearts with Scripture.

O **Action item:** Choose a passage of Scripture to memorize or meditate on throughout this week.

Take a moment to consider: Are your thoughts full of virtue and praise? Or might your thinking actually be feeding your stressful feelings?

O **Action item:** Consider these questions and answer them honestly. If you need help assessing yourself, ask someone who knows you well to tell you what your words and behaviors reveal to them about the condition of your thought life.

Finally, practice "bringing into captivity every thought to the obedience of Christ" (2 Corinthians 10:5) by refocusing one or more of your recurrent thoughts that tend to create anger, fear, or distraction.

O **Action item:** For each of these thoughts, fill in the following:

Today I choose not to dwell on . . .

____

____

Instead, I will refocus my thoughts to dwell on . . .

____

____

STABILIZING YOUR SOUL

Psalm 46:10 exhorts us to "Be still, and know that I am God." Cultivating a quietness of soul by taking time to be still in God's presence is key to calming our anxiety and enabling us to respond to stressful circumstances with poise. But, as we approach the Lord in prayer, it can sometimes be difficult to quiet our minds. The pressure of stressful circumstances—especially those over which we have little or no control—can keep our minds and hearts racing. In such times, as we discussed in our lesson, we need to proactively turn each of our "cares into prayers."

What might this look like? Here are a few examples:

- Lord, I'm going in for chemo today. Please give me Your grace.
- Lord, I have to deal with this mechanical issue in my car. You know how much I used to rely on my husband for these things. But I trust You to provide for me and help me describe the problem to a mechanic.
- Lord, I have this job interview today, and I'm anxious about how it might turn out. Please give me clarity of mind in the interview and guide my steps and provide for my needs whatever the outcome.

These kinds of prayers don't immediately change our circumstances, but they do call out for help to the One who can. And when we lift each of our cares up specifically to our Heavenly Father in this way, we open the door for His peace to begin to fill the anxious places in our hearts.

○ **Action item:** Make a list of the major "cares" you're facing right now. For each of these, turn them into a prayer, using the examples above as a model. Ask the Lord to give you His peace regarding each concern.

NOW THE GOD OF HOPE FILL YOU WITH ALL JOY AND PEACE IN BELIEVING, THAT YE MAY ABOUND IN HOPE, THROUGH THE POWER OF THE HOLY GHOST. (ROMANS 15:13)

11

LIVING WITH HOPE

WHEN I AM DISCOURAGED

Session Notes

Discussion

Devotional Readings

1. A Needed Hope
2. A Wise Hope
3. An Enduring Hope
4. A Fearless Hope
5. Longing for Home

Personal Application

LIVING WITH HOPE

*"Blessed be the God and Father of our Lord Jesus Christ, which according to his abundant
mercy hath begotten us again unto a lively hope by the resurrection of Jesus Christ from the
dead, 4 To an inheritance incorruptible, and undefiled, and that fadeth not away, reserved
in heaven for you, 5 Who are kept by the power of God through faith unto salvation ready
to be revealed in the last time. 6 Wherein ye greatly rejoice, though now for a season, if
need be, ye are in heaviness through manifold temptations: 7 That the trial of your faith,
being much more precious than of gold that perisheth, though it be tried with fire, might be
found unto praise and honour and glory at the appearing of Jesus Christ: 8 Whom having
not seen, ye love; in whom, though now ye see him not, yet believing, ye rejoice with joy
unspeakable and full of glory: 9 Receiving the end of your faith, even the salvation of your
souls."* (1 Peter 1:3–9)

INTRODUCTION

____

____

____

"Now the God of hope fill you with all joy and peace in believing, that ye may abound in hope, through the power of the Holy Ghost." (Romans 15:13)

"As sorrowful, yet alway rejoicing…" (2 Corinthians 6:10)

1. A Living HOPE

Definition: *Lively,* from Greek *zoa*—"to live, breathe, be among the living."

Through Salvation

*"But God, who is rich in mercy, for his great love wherewith he loved us, 5 Even
when we were dead in sins, hath quickened us together with Christ, (by grace ye
are saved;) 6 And hath raised us up together, and made us sit together in heavenly
places in Christ Jesus:"* (Ephesians 2:4–6)

Because of Christ's RESURRECTION

"Then said his wife unto him, Dost thou still retain thine integrity? curse God, and die." (Job 2:9)

"For I know that my redeemer liveth, and that he shall stand at the latter day upon the earth: 26 And though after my skin worms destroy this body, yet in my flesh shall I see God: 27 Whom I shall see for myself, and mine eyes shall behold, and not another; though my reins be consumed within me." (Job 19:25–27)

"But if there be no resurrection of the dead, then is Christ not risen: 14 And if Christ be not risen, then is our preaching vain, and your faith is also vain. 15 Yea, and we are found false witnesses of God; because we have testified of God that he raised up Christ: whom he raised not up, if so be that the dead rise not. 16 For if the dead rise not, then is not Christ raised: 17 And if Christ be not raised, your faith is vain; ye are yet in your sins. 18 Then they also which are fallen asleep in Christ are perished. 19 If in this life only we have hope in Christ, we are of all men most miserable. 20 But now is Christ risen from the dead, and become the firstfruits of them that slept." (1 Corinthians 15:13–20)

2. A FUTURE HOPE

"To an inheritance incorruptible, and undefiled, and that fadeth not away, reserved in heaven for you," (1 Peter 1:4)

Heaven Is REAL

"Let not your heart be troubled: ye believe in God, believe also in me. 2 In my Father's house are many mansions: if it were not so, I would have told you. I go to prepare a place for you. 3 And if I go and prepare a place for you, I will come again, and receive you unto myself; that where I am, there ye may be also." (John 14:1–3)

"We are confident, I say, and willing rather to be absent from the body, and to be present with the Lord." (2 Corinthians 5:8)

"For the Lord himself shall descend from heaven with a shout, with the voice of the archangel, and with the trump of God: and the dead in Christ shall rise first: 17 Then we which are alive and remain shall be caught up together with them in the clouds, to meet the Lord in the air: and so shall we ever be with the Lord." (1 Thessalonians 4:16–17)

*"In a moment, in the twinkling of an eye, at the last trump: for the trumpet
shall sound, and the dead shall be raised incorruptible, and we shall be changed.
53 For this corruptible must put on incorruption, and this mortal must put on
immortality. 54 So when this corruptible shall have put on incorruption, and this
mortal shall have put on immortality, then shall be brought to pass the saying that
is written, Death is swallowed up in victory." (1 Corinthians 15:52–54)*

*"And I saw a new heaven and a new earth: for the first heaven and the first earth
were passed away; and there was no more sea. 2 And I John saw the holy city, new
Jerusalem, coming down from God out of heaven, prepared as a bride adorned for her
husband. 3 And I heard a great voice out of heaven saying, Behold, the tabernacle of
God is with men, and he will dwell with them, and they shall be his people, and God
himself shall be with them, and be their God. 4 And God shall wipe away all tears from
their eyes; and there shall be no more death, neither sorrow, nor crying, neither shall
there be any more pain: for the former things are passed away." (Revelation 21:1–4)*

Heaven Is ~~PERFECT~~ ~~REAL~~ PERFECT

"And there shall in no wise enter into it any thing that defileth, neither whatsoever worketh abomination, or maketh a lie: but they which are written in the Lamb's book of life." (Revelation 21:27)

Heaven Is ~~PERFECT~~ ETERNAL

*"For the creature was made subject to vanity, not willingly, but by reason of him
who hath subjected the same in hope, 21 Because the creature itself also shall be
delivered from the bondage of corruption into the glorious liberty of the children of
God." (Romans 8:20–21)*

Heaven Is RESERVED

*"We give thanks to God and the Father of our Lord Jesus Christ, praying always for
you, 4 Since we heard of your faith in Christ Jesus, and of the love which ye have to
all the saints, 5 For the hope which is laid up for you in heaven, whereof ye heard
before in the word of the truth of the gospel;" (Colossians 1:3–5)*

*"To an inheritance incorruptible, and undefiled, and that fadeth not away, reserved
in heaven for you, 5 Who are kept by the power of God through faith unto salvation
ready to be revealed in the last time." (1 Peter 1:4–5)*

"For the which cause I also suffer these things: nevertheless I am not ashamed: for I know whom I have believed, and am persuaded that he is able to keep that which I have committed unto him against that day." (2 Timothy 1:12)

3. A daley HOPE

HEAVINESS Is for a Season

"Wherein ye greatly rejoice, though now for a season, if need be, ye are in heaviness through manifold temptations:" (1 Peter 1:6)

"For our light affliction, which is but for a moment, worketh for us a far more exceeding and eternal weight of glory; 18 While we look not at the things which are seen, but at the things which are not seen: for the things which are seen are temporal; but the things which are not seen are eternal." (2 Corinthians 4:17–18)

"That the trial of your faith, being much more precious than of gold that perisheth, though it be tried with fire, might be found unto praise and honour and glory at the appearing of Jesus Christ:" (1 Peter 1:7)

"But the God of all grace, who hath called us unto his eternal glory by Christ Jesus, after that ye have suffered a while, make you perfect, stablish, strengthen, settle you." (1 Peter 5:10)

HELP Is Available

"Whom having not seen, ye love; in whom, though now ye see him not, yet believing, ye rejoice with joy unspeakable and full of glory:" (1 Peter 1:8)

*"Who shall separate us from the love of Christ? shall tribulation, or distress, or persecution, or famine, or nakedness, or peril, or sword? 36 As it is written, For thy sake we are killed all the day long; we are accounted as sheep for the slaughter.
37 Nay, in all these things we are more than conquerors through him that loved us.
38 For I am persuaded, that neither death, nor life, nor angels, nor principalities, nor powers, nor things present, nor things to come, 39 Nor height, nor depth, nor any other creature, shall be able to separate us from the love of God, which is in Christ Jesus our Lord." (Romans 8:35–39)*

SIX SOURCES OF HOPE FOR GRIEVING CHRISTIANS

1. *The Word of God*

"Remember the word unto thy servant, upon which thou hast
caused me to hope. . . . 81 My soul fainteth for thy salvation: but I
hope in thy word." (Psalm 119:49, 81)

2. *Prayer*

"Casting all your care upon him; for he careth for you." (1 Peter 5:7)

3. *Praise*

"But I will hope continually, and will yet praise thee more and more." (Psalm 71:14)

4. *Confidence in God's purposes*

"For I know the thoughts that I think toward you, saith the LORD, thoughts of peace, and not of evil, to give you an expected end." (Jeremiah 29:11)

5. *The fellowship and testimonies of other Christians*

"I waited patiently for the LORD; and he inclined unto me, and heard
my cry. 2 He brought me up also out of an horrible pit, out of the
miry clay, and set my feet upon a rock, and established my goings.
3 And he hath put a new song in my mouth, even praise unto
our God: many shall see it, and fear, and shall trust in the LORD."
(Psalm 40:1–3)

6. *Looking forward to seeing Christ face to face*

"Whom having not seen, ye love; in whom, though now ye see him
not, yet believing, ye rejoice with joy unspeakable and full of glory:
9 Receiving the end of your faith, even the salvation of your souls."
(1 Peter 1:8–9)

CONCLUSION

___

___

___

GROUP DISCUSSION

1. Was there anything from last week's devotionals or application exercises that was particularly meaningful or helpful to you? What passage of Scripture has been most reassuring to you this past week?

2. What is the difference between hope and optimism? Do you think the difference matters in grief?

3. What are some practical ways in which we can help ourselves remember the eternal realities of Heaven in our day-to-day lives?

4. What are some of the challenges associated with maintaining hope in the face of grief? If you feel comfortable doing so, share with the group any specific struggles you're experiencing in this area, so they can pray for you.

5. What is one way the group can pray for you as it relates to grief this week? (A prayer request section is included at the end of this workbook so you can record the requests of other group members.)

SESSION ELEVEN: DAY ONE

A NEEDED HOPE

Hope deferred maketh the heart sick: but when the desire cometh, it is a tree of life. (Proverbs 13:12)

It has been said that a man can live forty days without food, three days without water, and eight minutes without air. But he can only live for one second without hope.

Hope—the belief that things can improve for us, and that there is a real pathway for that improvement to happen[1]—has been linked to improved health, socioeconomic, and other life outcomes across a variety of human age cohorts.[2] Unfortunately, a lack of hope has become endemic in our society, leading to a surge in depression, anxiety, and other adverse social consequences.[3]

We need hope. Of course, this is not a new insight. Long ago, the writer of Proverbs observed, "Hope deferred maketh the heart sick: but when the desire cometh, it is a tree of life" (Proverbs 13:12). Our souls need hope as much as our bodies need air. We cannot survive without it.

Where do we find our hope? For the people of God, our hope is found in the Lord. As Psalm 33:20–22 puts it, "Our soul waiteth for the LORD: he is our help and our shield. For our heart shall rejoice in him, because we have trusted in his holy name. Let thy mercy, O LORD, be upon us, according as we hope in thee."

The *basis* of our hope, then, is God Himself—His perfect, unchanging nature and His unshakeable love for us. And the *content* of our hope is drawn from His eternal, unbreakable promises to us.

Among the many promises of God to us are those related to eternal life—the life *after* this one—that God invites us, His children, to spend with Him. Though the Bible tells us with great certainty that Heaven is the eternal destination of the children of God, it does not give us extensive detail or description of Heaven. We catch glimpses of it (see, for example, Revelation 21:1–3), but the fullness of the glory and majesty of Heaven is not possible to put into words.

But what we do know is that Heaven—our true home—is *real*. And this is true regardless of what our present circumstances, emotions, fears, or grief might tell us. Heaven is real even when we forget to hope in it. It is as real as the sunrise that happens whether or not we think about it. It is as real as the ocean tides that come in and go out, even when their existence is far from our minds.

This is the stuff of hope—*real* hope, the kind of hope that satisfies and enables us to keep moving forward even in our season of grief. When we find ourselves needing hope, we would do well to remind ourselves of the glorious future that God has promised for us as His beloved children.

TODAY'S TAKEAWAY

Remembering the eternal realities of Heaven can flame our hope and strengthen our resolve to press forward for Christ here and now.

JOURNAL PROMPT

How can remembering the eternal realities of Heaven help you to deal with the fact that some of your past or current hopes may be deferred or, ultimately, not realized at all?

SESSION ELEVEN: DAY TWO

A WISE HOPE

If in this life only we have hope in Christ, we are of all men most miserable. But now is Christ risen from the dead, and become the firstfruits of them that slept. (1 Corinthians 15:19–20)

On April 1, 1998, the Burger King corporation took out a full-page advertisement in *USA Today* promoting a "Left-Handed Whopper," designed with the thirty-two million left-handed Americans in mind. The burger came complete with "all condiments rotated 180 degrees, thereby redistributing the weight of the sandwich so that the bulk of the condiments will skew to the left, thereby reducing the amount of lettuce and other toppings from spilling out the right side of the burger." Additionally, the upper bun featured "sesame seeds meticulously placed to ensure [the] least amount of loss during consumption, favoring left-handed eating technique," and the lower bun was "realigned to compensate for [the] shift in weight." This sandwich was, according to Burger King's then-vice president of marketing, the "ultimate 'HAVE IT YOUR WAY' for our left-handed customers."[4]

As you've probably already guessed, all of this was an elaborate April Fool's Day prank. But that didn't stop thousands of left-handed people from getting in line at Burger King to request their specially designed burger. And of course, "they had to wait in line behind right-handed folks equally caught up with making sure they got the correct Whopper."[5]

No doubt some of these customers felt a bit foolish when they realized they had fallen for an April Fool's joke.

When it comes to our hopes for the future, we may sometimes wonder if we've been "played," if we are in fact fools for believing as we do. In particular, the hope of the resurrection—of one day spending eternity face to face with Jesus—may seem at times like a far-fetched, foolish dream, or (at least) of little relevance to our current circumstances.

In 1 Corinthians 15, the apostle Paul writes to people who need reassurance about their future, both short-term and long-term. You can be *certain* that you will share in the resurrection of the dead unto life, he tells them. Why? Because Christ Himself rose from the dead, thereby becoming "the firstfruits of them that slept" (1 Corinthians 15:20). If this weren't true, he says, we would have hope "in this life only" and would be "of all men most miserable" (1 Corinthians 15:19). But since He *has* in fact risen from the dead, we can join Paul in proclaiming, "thanks be to God, which giveth us the victory through our Lord Jesus Christ"!

Sometimes, when we put our trust or hope in something or someone, we are left feeling foolish. But when we put our hope and trust in God and His promises, we will never—*can* never—be put to shame. Jesus' resurrection secures our eternal future with Him. God's promises never fail.

TODAY'S TAKEAWAY

When we are tempted to question our hopes for the future, especially the eternal future that God has promised to us, we need to remember that our trust is in Jesus—the One who is Wisdom itself—whose resurrection secures and guarantees our future with Him.

JOURNAL PROMPT

Do you sometimes wonder if you're foolish to believe the things you do, especially about the "life hereafter" with Jesus? If so, ask Him to reassure your heart of the certainty of His promises to you.

SESSION ELEVEN: DAY THREE

AN ENDURING HOPE

And God shall wipe away all tears from their eyes; and there shall be no more death, neither sorrow, nor crying, neither shall there be any more pain: for the former things are passed away. (Revelation 21:4)

On a recent tour of church history sites in England that I led, we visited the site of Charles Spurgeon's tomb.[6] Charles Haddon Spurgeon (1834–1892) was a nineteenth century English preacher, pastor, teacher, founder of orphanages and a college, author, supporter of cross-cultural missions and evangelism, and a staunch opponent of slavery. His writing output was prodigious, encompassing a great number of "sermons, an autobiography, commentaries, books on prayer, devotionals, magazines, poetry, and hymns." By the time he died in 1892, "he had preached nearly 3,600 sermons and published 49 volumes of commentaries, sayings, anecdotes, illustrations, and devotions."[7] It's estimated that over the course of his lifetime, Spurgeon had preached the gospel to more than ten million people.

These accomplishments did not come easy, however. Throughout his life, Spurgeon suffered from painful chronic health conditions, including gout, kidney disease, and recurring bouts of depression. And he died at the relatively young age of fifty-seven. But despite the continual pain with which he struggled, Spurgeon took hope from the words of Revelation 21:4, which tell us that "God shall wipe away all tears from their eyes; and there shall be no more death, neither sorrow, nor crying, neither shall there be any more pain: for the former things are passed away." These very words, in fact, are engraved on the front of Spurgeon's tomb.

What gave Spurgeon strength to go on was knowing that one day he would be in the immediate presence of God—the One who would, *personally*, wipe away his tears. This is what makes the promise of Heaven so wonderful. The glory and beauty of Heaven is not merely in its golden streets or crystal clear river or wall made of precious stones or gates of pearls. The glory and beauty of Heaven is the presence of God Himself. All of eternity will be spent in the place where He is. The cares and pains and heartaches of the world will be left behind and forgotten. The need for fervent and urgent prayer will be replaced. The longing so many feel for purpose and meaning will be met by the presence of God. We will no longer need clocks and calendars, for time will reach an end. We will never need a light, for Jesus is the constant and unchanging light of Heaven. This is our eternal home.

When we know that the pain we are currently experiencing won't last forever—that there is a home with God awaiting us, a future in which every tear will be wiped away—we are empowered to endure our suffering with genuine hope.

TODAY'S TAKEAWAY

Hope—true, *biblical hope*—provides us with the endurance we need in the face of our current pain and suffering.

JOURNAL PROMPT

What are the areas of your life in which you need to endure right now? Ask the Lord to fill you with hope regarding these things, and to enable you to endure them with hope.

SESSION ELEVEN: DAY FOUR

A FEARLESS HOPE

Jesus said unto her, I am the resurrection, and the life: he that believeth in me, though he were dead, yet shall he live: And whosoever liveth and believeth in me shall never die. Believest thou this? (John 11:25–26)

Grief, especially when it's caused by the loss of a loved one, can fuel fears of our own death. But the Bible makes it clear that for the Christian, death—while still an enemy—is a *defeated* enemy: "O death, where is thy sting? O grave, where is thy victory? The sting of death is sin; and the strength of sin is the law. But thanks be to God, which giveth us the victory through our Lord Jesus Christ" (1 Corinthians 15:55–57).

Our ultimate victory over death was secured by Jesus' resurrection from the dead. Knowing where His mission would take Him—to the cross and the empty tomb—Jesus was able to confidently say, "I am the resurrection, and the life: he that believeth in me, though he were dead, yet shall he live: And whosoever liveth and believeth in me shall never die" (John 11:25–26).

Grasping the truth of this reality can profoundly shape our perspective on our own eventual physical death. The great American evangelist and revivalist preacher D. L. Moody (1837–1899) once wrote,

> *Some day you will read in the papers that D. L. Moody, of East Northfield, is dead. Don't you believe a word of it! At that moment I shall be more alive than I am now. I shall have gone up higher, that is all; gone out of this old clay tenement into a house that is immortal, a body that death cannot touch, that sin cannot taint, a body like unto His own glorious body. I was born of the flesh in 1837. I was born of the Spirit in 1856. That which is born of the flesh may die. That which is born of the Spirit will live forever.*

First John 4:18 tells us that "There is no fear in love; but perfect love casteth out fear." Of course, the only love that can truly overcome all our fears is the love of God for His children. And, as it turns out, it is out of the abundance of His love for us that He promises us an eternal home with Him. When we find ourselves struggling with fear during our season of grief, then, the key to counteracting those fears is to remind ourselves of our Heavenly Father's love-driven promises to us, and the fact that Jesus' resurrection guarantees our reservation in Heaven.

TODAY'S TAKEAWAY

Ultimately, the future holds no fear for the child of God who is living in faith and believing God's promises. God keeps all of His children, and our future with Him—guaranteed by the resurrection of Jesus from the dead—is settled and secure.

JOURNAL PROMPT

Are you struggling with fear of your own death? If so, lay that before the Lord and ask Him to show you in a fresh way how the resurrection of His Son guarantees your future with Him.

SESSION ELEVEN: DAY FIVE

LONGING FOR HOME

For here have we no continuing city, but we seek one to come. (Hebrews 13:14)

In 2013, Torbjørn "Thor" Pedersen left Denmark to visit every country in the world without flying, a challenge filled with deep personal meaning. Pedersen faced numerous obstacles including severe illness, logistical nightmares, and unexpected delays—most notably a two-year pause in Hong Kong due to the COVID-19 pandemic. Despite these hardships, he was driven by a profound longing for home. Reflecting on his journey, Pedersen shared, "Coming home is something I've been focusing on—something I've wanted to materialize for the longest time." This anticipation of returning home fueled his determination through the weary moments of his nearly decade-long adventure.[8]

Scripture describes us as pilgrims whose ultimate citizenship is in Heaven rather than here on Earth. Philippians 3:20, for example, tells us that "our conversation is in heaven; from whence also we look for the Saviour, the Lord Jesus Christ." The next verse goes on to tell us that our Savior, Jesus Christ, will one day "change our vile body, that it may be fashioned like unto his glorious body, according to the working whereby he is able even to subdue all things unto himself" (Philippians 3:21).

The author of the book of Hebrews spends considerable time discussing the superiority of Jesus Christ as the final, perfect sacrifice who completely fulfills the Old Testament law. In Hebrews 13:11–14, an analogy is drawn between the Old Testament sacrificial system and Jesus' sacrifice. Just as in the Old Testament the high priest would take the blood of sacrificial animals into the "sanctuary" (the Most Holy Place) while the animals' bodies were burned "without the camp," so "Jesus also, that he might sanctify the people with his own blood, suffered without the gate"—that is, at Golgotha, which was outside the city limits (Hebrews 13:11–12). In the next two verses, the writer of Hebrews draws an explicit connection between us and Jesus: just as Jesus willingly bore shame and disgrace on our behalf, we likewise should willingly bear the "reproach" of following Him (Hebrews 13:13). Why? Because our citizenship isn't here after all: it's in Heaven. Here, we have "no continuing city, but we seek one to come" (Hebrews 13:14).

In biblical times (and even in many places today), a city represented a place of security, of safety, of permanence. For us, though, no earthly city can provide the security, safety, or permanence that our future heavenly home does. We live our lives here on earth with what C. S. Lewis referred to as a "desire for our own far-off country," a longing that can only be fulfilled in Heaven.[9]

Grief reminds us, perhaps like nothing else, that this world is not our home. The good news is that for those whose faith is in Christ, that "desire for our own far-off country" *will* be fulfilled. "In my Father's house are many mansions," Jesus promises. "If it were not so, I would have told you. I go to prepare a place for you. And if I go and prepare a place for you, I will come again, and receive you unto myself; that where I am, there ye may be also" (John 14:2–3).

TODAY'S TAKEAWAY

The hope of one day arriving in the "far-off country" where our Lord has prepared a home for us can fuel our determination and tenacity as we walk through the weary moments of our season of grief.

JOURNAL PROMPT

How does knowing that this life is not all there is shape or change your perspective on the grief and sorrow you're currently experiencing?

PERSONAL APPLICATION

The following exercises are intended to give you an opportunity to apply the things you're learning and discussing in the group meetings and daily devotionals. They don't have to be done in any particular sequence or on a particular day of the week. If you only have the physical or emotional energy to complete one of these exercises, that's fine. The point is to allow the Spirit of God to minister to your heart during this time of grief.

FINDING HOPE WHEN YOU FEEL DISCOURAGED

Life, especially during a season of grief, can be discouraging. But as we discussed in our lesson, there is help available to us on a daily basis—not just for the distant future, but for the here and now as well.

Today and tomorrow and every day until you see Jesus face to face, help is available to you. Our love for Christ and anticipation of seeing Him fuels our hope. But even before we see Him face to face, we have the assurance that God is with us in our present suffering.

There are six sources of daily hope to which we can cling when we're feeling discouraged and weighed down by grief.

1. *The Word of God* (Psalm 119:49, 81): We've seen repeatedly throughout this study that the promises of God give us hope.
2. *Prayer* (1 Peter 5:7): As we pour out our hearts to the Lord in prayer and cast our cares on Him, He renews our hope and assures us of His care.
3. *Praise* (Psalm 71:14): Praising God reminds us of His unchanging attributes. Thinking on His power, goodness, faithfulness, love, and more, fills our hearts with hope.

4. *Confidence in God's purposes* (Jeremiah 29:11): Sometimes in grief, we're tempted to think the significant potential for our life was lost with whoever or whatever it was we lost. But recognizing that God has a plan for our lives in this moment, that He has a future for us, and that He has good and wise purposes for what He is doing, provides hope.

5. *The fellowship and testimonies of other Christians* (Psalm 40:1–3): Being around others who hope in God and hearing the testimonies of others who have seen God work in hard places in their lives, strengthens our hope in God.

6. *Seeing Christ face to face* (1 Peter 1:8–9): Knowing that we will someday see Jesus face to face can fill us with joy and buoy our hope in times of discouragement.

○ **Action Item:** For each of the six sources of hope in the midst of discouragement listed above, take a few moments to brainstorm some specific ways you might be able to avail yourself of them when you're feeling discouraged. Some suggestive prompts are included here.

1. The Word of God
   I can remind myself of God's promises by . . .

   ____

   ____

2. Prayer
   The best setting for me to spend time in prayer is . . .

   ____

   ____

3. Praise
   I can remind myself of God's unchanging character by . . .

4. Confidence in God's purposes
   I can remind myself of God's good purposes for me by . . .

5. The fellowship and testimonies of other Christians
   One way that I can expose myself to the fellowship and testimonies of other Christians over this next week is . . .

6. Seeing Christ face to face
   Based on what Scripture tells me about Jesus, this is what I imagine it will be like to meet Jesus face to face:

Now, choose one of these methods of finding hope in the midst of discouragement and make a plan to use it the next time you're feeling discouraged.

TAKING INVENTORY OF YOUR HOPES

Going through a season of grief can impact our hopes in a variety of ways. Take a few moments to consider how your journey through grief has affected your hopes.

○ **Action item:** Write out your answers to the following questions and then spend some time in prayer talking with God about them.

What are some of the things you currently find yourself hoping for?

What do you hope to see as you look back on this season a year from now? Five years? Ten years?

How has your season of grief impacted your past or current hopes? Have any of them changed? If so, in what ways?

In a season of grief, it can seem like some (or many) of our hopes have been deferred or even foreclosed altogether. Are you wrestling with the reality that this may be true of some of your hopes? If so, identify them here and talk with God about them. Ask Him to replace your fears with His peace.

STABILIZING YOUR SOUL

Using the words of a psalm or a biblically-saturated hymn or poem in prayer can be powerful medicine for your soul during this season of grief. When you can't come up with the words to say yourself, let others who have gone before you lead the way into the caring presence of your Father.

○ **Action item:** Pray through these words of Psalm 33. There is space provided below to record your reflections.

Psalm 33

1 Rejoice in the LORD, O ye righteous: for praise is comely for the upright. 2 Praise
the LORD with harp: sing unto him with the psaltery and an instrument of ten
strings. 3 Sing unto him a new song; play skilfully with a loud noise. 4 For the word
of the LORD is right; and all his works are done in truth. 5 He loveth righteousness
and judgment: the earth is full of the goodness of the LORD. 6 By the word of the
LORD were the heavens made; and all the host of them by the breath of his mouth.
7 He gathereth the waters of the sea together as an heap: he layeth up the depth in
storehouses. 8 Let all the earth fear the LORD: let all the inhabitants of the world
stand in awe of him. 9 For he spake, and it was done; he commanded, and it stood
fast. 10 The LORD bringeth the counsel of the heathen to nought: he maketh the
devices of the people of none effect. 11 The counsel of the LORD standeth for ever,
the thoughts of his heart to all generations. 12 Blessed is the nation whose God
is the LORD; and the people whom he hath chosen for his own inheritance. 13 The
LORD looketh from heaven; he beholdeth all the sons of men. 14 From the place of
his habitation he looketh upon all the inhabitants of the earth. 15 He fashioneth
their hearts alike; he considereth all their works. 16 There is no king saved by the
multitude of an host: a mighty man is not delivered by much strength. 17 An horse
is a vain thing for safety: neither shall he deliver any by his great strength. 18
Behold, the eye of the LORD is upon them that fear him, upon them that hope in his
mercy; 19 To deliver their soul from death, and to keep them alive in famine. 20
Our soul waiteth for the LORD: he is our help and our shield. 21 For our heart shall
rejoice in him, because we have trusted in his holy name. 22 Let thy mercy, O LORD,
be upon us, according as we hope in thee.

YEA, THOUGH I WALK THROUGH THE VALLEY OF THE SHADOW OF DEATH, I WILL FEAR NO EVIL: FOR THOU ART WITH ME; THY ROD AND THY STAFF THEY COMFORT ME. (PSALM 23:4)

12

FOLLOWING THE GOOD SHEPHERD

WHEN I DON'T KNOW THE FUTURE

Session Notes

Discussion

Devotional Readings

1. Through
2. Trusting the Shepherd
3. Drinking Water in the Valley
4. Walking with Resilience
5. The Oil of Gladness

Personal Application

FOLLOWING THE GOOD SHEPHERD

"The L*ORD is my shepherd; I shall not want.* 2 *He maketh me to lie down in green pastures: he leadeth me beside the still waters.* 3 *He restoreth my soul: he leadeth me in the paths of righteousness for his name's sake.* 4 *Yea, though I walk through the valley of the shadow of death, I will fear no evil: for thou art with me; thy rod and thy staff they comfort me.* 5 *Thou preparest a table before me in the presence of mine enemies: thou anointest my head with oil; my cup runneth over.* 6 *Surely goodness and mercy shall follow me all the days of my life: and I will dwell in the house of the* L*ORD for ever."* (Psalm 23:1–6)

INTRODUCTION

____

____

____

1. THE PROVISION OF THE SHEPHERD

"The L*ORD is my shepherd . . ."* (Psalm 23:1)

"I am the good shepherd: the good shepherd giveth his life for the sheep. . . . 14 *I am the good shepherd, and know my sheep, and am known of mine.* 15 *As the Father knoweth me, even so know I the Father: and I lay down my life for the sheep."* (John 10:11, 14–15)

A- NOURISHMENT

"He maketh me to lie down in green pastures: he leadeth me beside the still waters." (Psalm 23:2)

"And Jesus said unto them, I am the bread of life: he that cometh to me shall never hunger; and he that believeth on me shall never thirst." (John 6:35)

"He that believeth on me, as the scripture hath said, out of his belly shall flow rivers of living water. 39 *(But this spake he of the Spirit, which they that believe on him should receive: for the Holy Ghost was not yet given; because that Jesus was not yet glorified.)"* (John 7:38–39)

B - REST

"Come unto me, all ye that labour and are heavy laden, and I will give you rest. 29
Take my yoke upon you, and learn of me; for I am meek and lowly in heart: and ye shall find rest unto your souls." (Matthew 11:28–29)

"For he that is entered into his rest, he also hath ceased from his own works, as God did from his." (Hebrews 4:10)

"It is vain for you to rise up early, to sit up late, to eat the bread of sorrows: for so he giveth his beloved sleep." (Psalm 127:2)

"I will both lay me down in peace, and sleep: for thou, LORD, only makest me dwell in safety." (Psalm 4:8)

"And he said, My presence shall go with thee, and I will give thee rest." (Exodus 33:14)

"Thou wilt keep him in perfect peace, whose mind is stayed on thee: because he
trusteth in thee. 4 Trust ye in the LORD for ever: for in the LORD JEHOVAH is everlasting strength:" (Isaiah 26:3–4)

"Trust in the LORD with all thine heart; and lean not unto thine own understanding." (Proverbs 3:5)

C - RESTORATION

"He restoreth my soul . . ." (Psalm 23:3)

"O my God, my soul is cast down within me . . ." (Psalm 42:6)

"What time I am afraid, I will trust in thee." (Psalm 56:3)

"From the end of the earth will I cry unto thee, when my heart is overwhelmed: lead me to the rock that is higher than I." (Psalm 61:2)

D - DIRECTION

". . . he leadeth me in the paths of righteousness for his name's sake" (Psalm 23:3)

"My sheep hear my voice, and I know them, and they follow me:" (John 10:27)

2. THE ~~PRESENCE~~ OF THE SHEPHERD

"Yea, though I walk through the valley of the shadow of death, I will fear no evil: for thou art with me; thy rod and thy staff they comfort me." (Psalm 23:4)

The REALity of Valleys

"Above all, taking the shield of faith, wherewith ye shall be able to quench all the fiery darts of the wicked." (Ephesians 6:16)

"Be sober, be vigilant; because your adversary the devil, as a roaring lion, walketh about, seeking whom he may devour:" (1 Peter 5:8)

The Path through the Valleys

"When thou passest through the waters, I will be with thee; and through the rivers, they shall not overflow thee: when thou walkest through the fire, thou shalt not be burned; neither shall the flame kindle upon thee." (Isaiah 43:2)

Quote: *"When we follow the Lord, we cannot fail to be on the right path."* —**David Gibson**

". . . for he hath said, I will never leave thee, nor forsake thee. 6 So that we may boldly say, The Lord is my helper, and I will not fear what man shall do unto me.." (Hebrews 13:5–6)

"Behold, God is mine helper: the Lord is with them that uphold my soul." (Psalm 54:4)

Quote: *"The comfort of the good shepherd's presence is all the more wonderful when we take seriously the reality of the darkness and the presence of evil. . . . The comfort is the presence of the shepherd in the midst of the danger rather than the comfort of the removal of the danger."*—**David Gibson**

"For there stood by me this night the angel of God, whose I am, and whom I serve, 24 Saying, Fear not, Paul; thou must be brought before Caesar: and, lo, God hath given thee all them that sail with thee. 25 Wherefore, sirs, be of good cheer: for I believe God, that it shall be even as it was told me." (Acts 27:23–25)

The Shepherd's ___CARE___ in the Valleys

"Yea, though I walk through the valley of the shadow of death, I will fear no evil: for thou art with me; thy rod and thy staff they comfort me." (Psalm 23:4)

"He delivered me from my strong enemy, and from them that hated me: for they were too strong for me. 19 They prevented me in the day of my calamity: but the LORD was my stay. 20 He brought me forth also into a large place: he delivered me, because he delighted in me." (2 Samuel 22:18–20)

"All we like sheep have gone astray; we have turned every one to his own way..." (Isaiah 53:6)

3. THE ___PROMISES___ OF THE SHEPHERD

"Thou preparest a table before me in the presence of mine enemies: thou anointest my head with oil; my cup runneth over. 6 Surely goodness and mercy shall follow me all the days of my life: and I will dwell in the house of the LORD for ever." (Psalm 23:5–6)

___PROVISION___ in the Midst of Trouble

"Every good gift and every perfect gift is from above, and cometh down from the Father of lights, with whom is no variableness, neither shadow of turning." (James 1:17)

"Blessed be the God and Father of our Lord Jesus Christ, who hath blessed us with all spiritual blessings in heavenly places in Christ:" (Ephesians 1:3)

___PROSPECTS___ as Great as His Promises

Quote: *"The future is as bright as the promises of God."*—**Adoniram Judson**

"Surely goodness and mercy shall follow me all the days of my life: and I will dwell in the house of the LORD for ever." (Psalm 23:6)

"For all the promises of God in him are yea, and in him Amen, unto the glory of God by us." (2 Corinthians 1:20)

"He that spared not his own Son, but delivered him up for us all, how shall he not with him also freely give us all things?" (Romans 8:32).

CONCLUSION

GROUP DISCUSSION

1. Was there anything from last week's devotionals or application exercises that was particularly meaningful or helpful to you? What passage of Scripture has been most reassuring to you this past week?

2. What are some of the challenges or obstacles to finding rest—whether physical, mental, emotional, or spiritual—during a season of grief? What are some strategies for overcoming these barriers?

3. What are some of the things from which we need protection or deliverance during our journey through the "valley of the shadow of death"?

4. In what ways has the Lord's goodness and mercy "followed" you during your season of grief?

5. What is one way the group can pray for you as it relates to grief this week? (A prayer request section is included at the end of this workbook so you can record the requests of other group members.)

SESSION TWELVE: DAY ONE

THROUGH

When thou passest through the waters, I will be with thee; and through the rivers, they shall not overflow thee: when thou walkest through the fire, thou shalt not be burned; neither shall the flame kindle upon thee. (Isaiah 43:2)

On December 4, 2017, the largest wildfire in California history—the Thomas Fire—erupted in Ventura and Santa Barbara Counties, ultimately burning more than 281,000 acres and destroying 1,000 structures.

One month later, in the early morning hours of January 9, 2018, a strong winter storm pummeled the region with upwards of 1.5 inches per hour of rain for multiple hours. In Montecito, California, the water-logged land, already unstable and full of debris from the Thomas Fire, gave way, triggering a massive mudslide that claimed twenty-three lives. Houses, possessions, people, and lifetimes of memories were swept away instantly under the powerful weight of a fifteen-foot-deep river of mud that devastated an entire community.[1]

Fires and raging waters are powerful and destructive, and they can wipe out everything and everyone in their path. Similarly, grief and the circumstances that cause it can feel like forces of nature coming to destroy all that is good and beautiful in our lives.

As we "pass through the waters and the fire" it can seem never-ending—like we will never get through to a life of safety and calm. And when we hear the sound of waters nearby, we may find ourselves fearing that the rivers of grief will once again rise to engulf or overwhelm us.

But the reality is that although our time in the "valley of the shadow of death" sometimes includes experiencing the fire and the raging waters, the path we are on continues *through* the valley to the mountain pastures beyond.

In Isaiah 43:1–3, the Lord tells his people Israel, "Fear not: for I have redeemed thee, I have called thee by thy name; thou art mine . . . I am the Lord thy God, the Holy One of Israel, thy Saviour." *Because* I have saved and redeemed you, He says, "when thou passest through the waters, I will be with thee; and through the rivers, they shall not overflow thee: when thou walkest through the fire, thou shalt not be burned; neither shall the flame kindle upon thee" (Isaiah 43:2).

The same is as true for us today as it was for the people of Israel: the Lord has saved and redeemed us. Therefore, no matter what circumstances He might allow to enter our lives, He will bring us *through*. We will not drown. We will not ultimately be destroyed.

Remember that grief is a journey, but it is not the final destination. The destination is still ahead. The Lord has promised that He will never leave nor forsake us (Hebrews 13:5–6, Psalm 54:4). And although we cannot always perceive the presence of the Lord in the midst of the journey, He is always with us—leading and guiding us . . . *through*.

TODAY'S TAKEAWAY

Even in the midst of the raging waters of grief, you can trust the Lord to be present in your life to lead and guide you to a place of hope and peace.

JOURNAL PROMPT

Are there times when it still feels like your life is being destroyed and you are drowning? Remind yourself of how you know that God is still leading you *through* by journaling how He has made His presence known to you in the past few days or weeks.

SESSION TWELVE: DAY TWO

TRUSTING THE SHEPHERD

The Lord is my shepherd; I shall not want. (Psalm 23:1)

When our journey of grief brings us into the valley, we have a Shepherd who has promised to lead us through it. Our responsibility is to choose to follow that Shepherd, to allow Him to lead us even when the path is dark, unpleasant, or frightening.

We make this choice, first of all, by intentionally trusting our good Shepherd. In particular, we make a choice to trust in His presence, protection, and provision.

Throughout Scripture, one of the most common refrains is the command to not be afraid. "Fear thou not; for I am with thee," the Lord says in Isaiah 41. "Be not dismayed; for I am thy God: I will strengthen thee; yea, I will help thee; yea, I will uphold thee with the right hand of my righteousness" (Isaiah 41:10).

Although David at times felt fear, he recognized that with the Lord as his Shepherd, he had no ultimate cause for fear. Why? Because he knew that the Lord was with him: "Yea, though I walk through the valley of the shadow of death, I will fear no evil: for thou art with me; thy rod and thy staff they comfort me" (Psalm 23:4).

Similarly, when we find ourselves in the valley of grief, we can know with certainty that the Lord is with us. He is not distant or aloof; instead, He is "a very present help in trouble" (Psalm 46:1). Irrespective of our feelings—whether we feel afraid or at peace in any given moment—our Shepherd is always present. Our feelings may change, but thank God, He never changes (Hebrews 13:8).

Because of our good Shepherd's continual presence with us, we can also rest confidently in His ongoing protection and provision at every step along the way. To be sure, it's important to be clear about what this does and doesn't mean. Although we will not always have everything we might want in a given moment, we'll always have exactly what we need to accomplish

God's purposes. And while living in a sinful, broken world means that we will sometimes be on the receiving end of exceedingly painful, heartbreaking, or tragic circumstances, the evil of this world cannot ultimately defeat us. Because we are "in Christ Jesus" (1 Corinthians 1:30), we are secure in our relationship with God and in our eternal destiny. His presence with us is our protection and provision.

We don't know exactly when David wrote the twenty-third Psalm—whether it was when he was young or later on in his life. But we do know that David was a shepherd before he was a king. And we know he was a shepherd who took his responsibility seriously. The good news for us as we walk through our own valley of grief is that our Shepherd is Jesus Christ Himself. Not only does He take that role seriously, He also fulfills it perfectly. He truly is the good Shepherd—and we can trust Him completely.

TODAY'S TAKEAWAY

We can trust our good Shepherd because He is always with us. His very presence in our lives is our protection and provision.

JOURNAL PROMPT

What has God protected you from in the midst of your suffering? What provisions has God blessed you with that remind you of His care for you?

SESSION TWELVE: DAY THREE

DRINKING WATER IN THE VALLEY

He sendeth the springs into the valleys, which run among the hills. (Psalm 104:10)

Following our good Shepherd through the valley of grief involves trusting the Shepherd (which we discussed yesterday). It also means being willing to drink water in the valley.

For all the terrors of the valley of the shadow of death, one thing that valleys often hold is water. It's part of the reason that shepherds lead their flocks through valleys to the mountains.

Our good Shepherd, the Lord Himself, "leadeth [us] beside still waters" (Psalm 23:2)—the very waters that He lovingly placed in the valley through which He now leads us. Psalm 104:10–11 says, "He sendeth the springs into the valleys, which run among the hills. They give drink to every beast of the field: the wild asses quench their thirst."

A good shepherd leads his sheep to the water that they need. But if the sheep do not drink the water in the valley, they will not get through.

God has graciously provided His Word, His Spirit, and His people to us—and these things are as available during seasons of grief as at any other time. In fact, they often become even more precious and meaningful to us in our grief.

- *God's Word:* In the pages of God's Word, we find timeless truths that transcend our immediate circumstances—truths about who God is and who we are in relationship to Him, truths about how the events of our lives (confusing or painful as they may be) fit into God's larger kingdom program. That is why, as we've emphasized so many times throughout this study, it's important to intentionally keep Scripture coming into our hearts and minds even when we don't emotionally relate to it or feel direct benefit from it. Like water for our bodies, so is God's Word for our souls: we cannot live without it.

- *God's Spirit:* In addition to illuminating His Word, applying it to our lives, and empowering us to live it out on a daily basis, God's Spirit continually assures us that we are forever His: "The Spirit itself beareth witness with our spirit, that we are the children of God" (Romans 8:16). What more comforting words could there possibly be for us during a time of grief?

- *God's People:* God uses His people to minister His love and comfort to us during our season of grief, to lighten our load through shared burden-carrying, and, when needed, to help keep us on "paths of righteousness" (Psalm 23:3) through wise counsel and sage advice.

Our good Shepherd provides for us in limitless supply through these gifts because He loves us. He nourishes our souls through His Word, hydrates our souls by His Spirit, and refreshes our souls through His people.

TODAY'S TAKEAWAY

As we walk through the valley of grief, it's crucial that we drink deeply of the waters in the valley that He has provided for us along the way.

JOURNAL PROMPT

Of the three provisions mentioned above, which has been most real to you in this past week? Which are you longing for and need the Lord to help lead you to?

SESSION TWELVE: DAY FOUR

WALKING WITH RESILIENCE

Looking unto Jesus the author and finisher of our faith . . . (Hebrews 12:2)

In an earlier session we looked at the importance of resilience—the ability to endure a difficult circumstance and come out of it with strength and confidence, stretched but still intact. As we walk through the valley of the shadow of death, we rely in part on the resilience that the Lord has already built into our lives. And of course, going through the valley is itself a resilience-building experience. That's important because even beyond the valley, resilience will be called for as you continue to walk the journey of grief.

When I think of someone who consistently lived a resilient life, I think of my mom, Maxine Chappell, who went to be with the Lord in 2020. She was an amazing mother, wife, soulwinner, educator, missionary, and more. She had been battling Alzheimer's for several years toward the end of her life, and after she had passed, I could only imagine the delight she experienced when she again recognized a face . . . and it was Jesus.

When you're a child, you don't fully appreciate the challenges your parents face. And when you're an adult, they don't always share them with you. Mom certainly experienced her share of losses and difficulties, some of which I wasn't aware of at the time. But even in those times of heartache, she never lost her focus on Christ.

How did she keep her eyes on the Lord? She walked with God and spent time in His Word, lived with gratitude, exercised faith, forgave those who wronged her, nurtured a vibrant prayer life, and trusted the Lord through the blessings and the losses. Through all of this, she left a legacy of a resilient life.

When our grief, fears, and anxieties threaten to overcome us, what we need is resilience. A resilient faith leads to a resilient life.

In his allegorical work *The Pilgrim's Progress*, John Bunyan paints a picture of the resilient life. Bunyan's main character, Christian, at one point finds his path leading through the Valley of the Shadow of Death—a place "exceedingly miry," filled with darkness so thick that Christian "could not see before him."

As Christian gingerly works his way through this landscape, he hears dreadful sounds and voices that threaten to overwhelm his spirit. "Fiends" and demons attempt to thwart Christian's path with discouraging thoughts and fears.

But in the midst of Christian's terror, he hears the words, "though I walk through the valley of the Shadow of Death, I will fear no ill, for thou art with me." This biblical echo strengthens Christian's heart and emboldens him to press on resolutely, declaring, "I will walk in the strength of the Lord God."

For the Christian, the resilient life comes as we look to Jesus—our Good Shepherd. He is the giver and supplier of the resilient life. He is the one who promised to give you the power to overcome. He is able to uphold and sustain you through any challenge or difficulty. He can enable you to walk in His strength and to finish your course with joy.

TODAY'S TAKEAWAY

The key to living a resilient life in the face of grief is to keep our eyes focused on Jesus, "the author and finisher of our faith" (Hebrews 12:2).

JOURNAL PROMPT

Can you see ways in which you've developed resilience in the past or in your current season of grief? If so, record them here and let that recognition be a source of encouragement to you. Then, write down one specific thing you can do over this next week to help you (continue to) keep your eyes fixed on Jesus.

SESSION TWELVE: DAY FIVE

THE OIL OF GLADNESS

. . . thou anointest my head with oil; . . . (Psalm 23:5)

"Thou anointest my head with oil," David says in Psalm 23:5. In using this language, he paints a striking picture. In the same way that a shepherd anoints a sheep's head to soothe its cuts, scrapes, and other wounds and to protect it from insects, so our Shepherd anoints our heads as a way of binding up our wounds and protecting us from further injury. Psalm 147:3 says, "He healeth the broken in heart, and bindeth up their wounds." Our good Shepherd leads us to a place of healing.

But there is more. In the Bible, anointing oil is often associated with gladness. For example, in Psalm 45:7, we find these words: "Thou lovest righteousness, and hatest wickedness: therefore God, thy God, hath anointed thee with the oil of gladness above thy fellows" (Psalm 45:7). When the good Shepherd anoints his sheep with oil, He brings them into a place of joy.

The interesting thing is that this sort of joy and gladness is compatible with the experience of grief and sorrow. How do we know this? Hebrews 1:9 makes it clear that the words of Psalm 45:7 were actually a messianic prophecy about Jesus. Think about this, then: Jesus, who was "a man of sorrows, and acquainted with grief" (Isaiah 53:3), was also full of the joy of the Lord. So, grief and joy are not incompatible opposites. Rather, we can experience the joy of Jesus even in the midst of our grief.

Biblically, anointing someone's head with oil also often signifies bestowing honor upon an individual (frequently in conjunction with a specific commission for service, for example as a king or prophet). Here, in Psalm 23, the good Shepherd—who now also takes on a Kingly role as well—anoints His sheep before inviting them to take seats of honor at the banquet table that He, the conquering Shepherd-King, has prepared for his guests. Of course, this picture does not come to full fruition until the great "marriage supper of the Lamb" described in Revelation 19:9. But even in this life, while we still experience the pain and sorrow of grief, our good Shepherd invites us to sit with Him at His table, enjoying His presence as His honored guests. In the midst of this broken, sinful world, the mercy and grace of God shine upon us as He lavishly provides the strength and sustenance we need.

As we go through our current season of grief, we can rest assured that "weeping may endure for a night, but joy cometh in the morning" (Psalm 30:5). And because of that promise, we can be grateful for the small moments of joy that penetrate our sad and lonely days, knowing that a full, lasting, and permanent joy awaits in the future.

TODAY'S TAKEAWAY

We can experience and even embrace the joy of Jesus in the midst of our grief, knowing that we can trust our good Shepherd to pour out His "oil of gladness"—healing, joy, and honor—upon us.

JOURNAL PROMPT

For this final journal entry, give yourself permission to enjoy the "oil of gladness." Take a few moments and, with a grateful heart, write out a few things that have been funny, beautiful, enjoyable, or have made you smile during this season of grief.

PERSONAL APPLICATION

This session's application exercises are designed to stimulate reflection on the Growing through Grief series as a whole. What are some of the things that have stood out to you along the way? What are the key things you want to remember? What points of application have you been prompted to consider? How are you different now than you were before you started this study? Take some time to work through one or more of the following exercises and record your insights here.

LOOKING BACK TO SEE AHEAD

Sometimes, it can be helpful to look backward in order to see the road ahead more clearly. As we conclude this series, it's worth taking some time to remember where we've been and what we've learned thus far along this journey of grief.

○ **Action Item:** Review the content of this study guide, focusing especially on the key points you want to remember from each session and the most important insights you've gained. Record them here to make it easier to recall these truths when you need them in the future. We've provided for you the primary biblical texts along with a brief summary and lesson takeaway for each session.

SESSION 1: UNDERSTANDING THE JOURNEY

- **Key Verse:** "Being confident of this very thing, that he which hath begun a good work in you will perform it until the day of Jesus Christ:" (Philippians 1:6)
- **Session Summary:** The grief, pain, and sorrow we experience in this life is a result of the introduction of sin into the world. But although grief is real, growth is possible. Through Jesus Christ, we have everything we need to grow in the mist of grief.

- **My key insights from this session:**

___

___

SESSION 2: SURRENDERING TO THE PROCESS: WHEN I WANT TO GIVE UP

- **Key Verse:** "But let patience have her perfect work, that ye may be perfect and entire, wanting nothing." (James 1:4)
- **Session Summary:** God uses our season of grief to develop faith and endurance in us. We participate with Him in that process by allowing patience to work in us, asking God for wisdom, and trusting Him to bring about spiritual maturity in our lives.
- **My key insights from this session:**

___

___

SESSION 3: RECEIVING GOD'S COMFORT: WHEN I AM HURTING

- **Key Verse:** "Blessed be God, even the Father of our Lord Jesus Christ, the Father of mercies, and the God of all comfort;" (2 Corinthians 1:3)
- **Session Summary:** God provides comfort through His Word, His Spirit, and His people—and above all, through His personal presence.
- **My key insights from this session:**

___

___

SESSION 4: RESTING IN GOD'S GOODNESS: WHEN I QUESTION GOD

- **Key Verse:** "For I know the thoughts that I think toward you, saith the LORD, thoughts of peace, and not of evil, to give you an expected end." (Jeremiah 29:11)

- **Session Summary:** God is powerful and sovereign, and He is always working His good purposes in our lives—even when we can't see what He's doing. Because of this, we can move forward with faith in the midst of our season of grief.

- **My key insights from this session:**

____

____

SESSION 5: RELYING ON THE HOLY SPIRIT: WHEN I DON'T KNOW WHAT TO DO

- **Key Verse:** "And this is the confidence that we have in him, that, if we ask any thing according to his will, he heareth us:" (1 John 5:14)

- **Session Summary:** During our season of grief, the Holy Spirit comes alongside us to provide the help we need. He aids us with our problems, assists us in our prayers, and directs our purpose.

- **My key insights from this session:**

____

____

SESSION 6: CLAIMING GOD'S PROMISE: WHEN I DON'T UNDERSTAND

- **Key Verse:** "And we know that all things work together for good to them that love God, to them who are the called according to his purpose." (Romans 8:28)

- **Session Summary:** As children of God, we can rest on the promise that God works all things—including our grief—together for our good and His glory by conforming us to the image of His Son, Jesus Christ.

- **My key insights from this session:**

____

____

SESSION 7: TRUSTING GOD'S FAITHFULNESS: WHEN I FEEL AFRAID

- **Key Verse:** "What time I am afraid, I will trust in thee. (Psalm 56:3)
- **Session Summary:** The fears we face during times of grief are real, but we can make decisions of trust that will yield a confidence of faith to carry us through this season.
- **My key insights from this session:**

___

___

SESSION 8: EMBRACING GOD'S GRACE: WHEN I FEEL WEAK

- **Key Verse:** "And he said unto me, My grace is sufficient for thee: for my strength is made perfect in weakness. Most gladly therefore will I rather glory in my infirmities, that the power of Christ may rest upon me." (2 Corinthians 12:9)
- **Session Summary:** God's grace is sufficient for our every need during a season of grief. It humbles us, strengthens us, purifies us, and empowers us, enabling us to do the will of God on a moment-by-moment basis.
- **My key insights from this session:**

___

___

SESSION 9: STAYING CONNECTED: WHEN I FEEL ALONE

- **Key Verse:** "For as we have many members in one body, and all members have not the same office: So we, being many, are one body in Christ, and every one members one of another." (Romans 12:4–5)

- **Session Summary:** Through the church, God has given believers a network of relationships to keep us connected to others during a time of grief. This network keeps us connected to life-giving truth, relationships, and opportunities for service.
- **My key insights from this session:**

____

____

SESSION 10: EXPERIENCING GOD'S PEACE: WHEN I AM STRESSED

- **Key Verse:** "And the peace of God, which passeth all understanding, shall keep your hearts and minds through Christ Jesus." (Philippians 4:7)
- **Session Summary:** We cannot always avoid the stresses associated with grief, but we can learn to think about and respond biblically to stress. We do this by intentionally rejoicing in the Lord, remembering His nearness, requesting His help, resting in Him, and reflecting on what is pleasing to Him.
- **My key insights from this session:**

____

____

SESSION 11: LIVING WITH HOPE: WHEN I AM DISCOURAGED

- **Key Verse:** "Now the God of hope fill you with all joy and peace in believing, that ye may abound in hope, through the power of the Holy Ghost." (Romans 15:13)
- **Session Summary:** Christian hope is based on the expectation that God will fulfill His promises. Through salvation in Christ and because of His resurrection, we have a living hope. We have a future hope of a home in Heaven that is real, perfect, eternal, and reserved for us. And we have a hope that is available to us on a daily basis as we go through the storms of grief.

- **My key insights from this session:**

____

____

SESSION 12: FOLLOWING THE GOOD SHEPHERD: WHEN I DON'T KNOW THE FUTURE

- **Key Verse:** "Yea, though I walk through the valley of the shadow of death, I will fear no evil: for thou art with me; thy rod and thy staff they comfort me." (Psalm 23:4)
- **Session Summary:** As we continue on our journey of grief, we can rest in the provision, presence, and promises of our Good Shepherd. As he leads us through the valley to the "green pastures" beyond, He provides us with nourishment, rest, restoration, and direction. All along, His presence protects us and gives us hope for a future of joy and gladness.
- **My key insights from this session:**

____

____

COMFORTING OTHERS WITH THE COMFORT THAT YOU HAVE RECEIVED

In an earlier session we said that the grief you're experiencing now will likely make it possible for you some day to be an encouragement to or otherwise serve someone else in their time of grief. We noted then that 2 Corinthians 1:3–4 tells us that receiving God's comfort personally equips us to comfort others: "Blessed be God, even the Father of our Lord Jesus Christ, the Father of mercies, and the God of all comfort; Who comforteth us in all our tribulation, that we may be able to comfort them which are in any trouble, by the comfort wherewith we ourselves are comforted of God."

The strength and opportunity to give this comfort to others doesn't always come right away. It may be sometime down the road for you. Even so, it's reassuring to know that, with God, nothing in our lives is wasted—not even this season of grief. In His timing, He can use it to bring blessing into your life and, through you, to bless others as well.

- ○ **Action item:** Take a few moments just to consider the possibilities—how might God use this season in your own life to bless others through you? Can you envision ways in which God might be preparing you for (eventual) service to others?

  Consider prayerfully the following suggestive categories and write down any possibilities that come to mind. Then, ask the Lord to show you which, if any, of these ideas He'd like you to pursue now.

1. ENCOURAGEMENT FROM SCRIPTURE

What passages of Scripture have been particularly meaningful or comforting to you during this season of grief? In what ways might they be encouraging to others?

Are there any passages of Scripture that you understand differently than before you entered into this time of grief? How might that new understanding be beneficial to someone else going through a similar period of grief?

Is there anyone that you know who needs a biblically-informed word of encouragement from you this week?

---

2. PRACTICAL HELP

What forms of practical assistance have been the most helpful to you during this time of grief?

____

____

Of these, are there any that you are in a position to be able to provide to others?

____

____

Is there anyone that you know specifically who has practical needs that you might be able to help meet?

____

____

STABILIZING YOUR SOUL

Your good Shepherd, Jesus Christ, has led you to the valley of grief, and He will also lead you through and beyond this valley. Along the way, He will provide you with the nourishment, rest, restoration, and direction you need. His promises for a future of joy and gladness are certain and guaranteed. And all the while, He is working to accomplish His good purposes in your life, bringing about spiritual maturity in you as He conforms you more and more into His image.

○ **Action item:** As you come to the conclusion of this series, take some time to reflect on your journey of grief thus far. Then, write out a prayer of praise, petition, and thanksgiving to your good Shepherd. Entrust your life into His loving care.

____

____

PRAYER REQUESTS

Use these pages to record the prayer requests shared by fellow group members. (Out of a respect for privacy, it may be best to write first names only.)

Date: **Request:**

Date: **Request:**

Date: **Request:**

Date: **Request:**

BIBLE PROMISES FOR GRIEVING CHRISTIANS

The following Scripture passages are encouraging promises from God's Word for times of grief. These are included as a resource for you to read, highlight, and turn to often. There is additional space provided at the end for you to add passages not listed here that God uses in your life and you would like to refer to in the future.

Yea, though I walk through the valley of the shadow of death, I will fear no evil: for thou art with me; thy rod and thy staff they comfort me. (Psalm 23:4)

Why art thou cast down, O my soul? and why art thou disquieted within me? hope in God: for I shall yet praise him, who is the health of my countenance, and my God. (Psalm 43:5)

What time I am afraid, I will trust in thee. (Psalm 56:3)

Trust in him at all times; ye people, pour out your heart before him: God is a refuge for us. Selah. (Psalm 62:8)

Sing forth the honour of his name: make his praise glorious. (Psalm 66:2)

But I will hope continually, and will yet praise thee more and more. (Psalm 71:14)

My flesh and my heart faileth: but God is the strength of my heart, and my portion for ever. (Psalm 73:26)

Therefore is my spirit overwhelmed within me; my heart within me is desolate. I remember the days of old; I meditate on all thy works; I muse on the work of thy hands. I stretch forth my hands unto thee: my soul thirsteth after thee, as a thirsty land. Selah. (Psalm 143:4–6)

Trust in the Lord with all thine heart; and lean not unto thine own understanding. In all thy ways acknowledge him, and he shall direct thy paths. (Proverbs 3:4–6)

Thou wilt keep him in perfect peace, whose mind is stayed on thee: because he trusteth in thee. Trust ye in the Lord for ever: for in the Lord Jehovah is everlasting strength: (Isaiah 26:3–4)

Why sayest thou, O Jacob, and speakest, O Israel, My way is hid from the Lord, and my judgment is passed over from my God? Hast thou not known? hast thou not heard, that the everlasting God, the Lord, the Creator of the ends of the earth, fainteth not, neither is weary? there is no searching of his understanding. He giveth power to the faint; and to them that have no might he increaseth strength. Even the youths shall faint and be weary, and the young men shall utterly fall: But they that wait upon the Lord shall renew their strength; they shall mount up with wings as eagles; they shall run, and not be weary; and they shall walk, and not faint. (Isaiah 40:27–31)

Fear thou not; for I am with thee: be not dismayed; for I am thy God: I will strengthen thee; yea, I will help thee; yea, I will uphold thee with the right hand of my righteousness. (Isaiah 41:10)

When thou passest through the waters, I will be with thee; and through the rivers, they shall not overflow thee: when thou walkest through the fire, thou shalt not be burned; neither shall the flame kindle upon thee. (Isaiah 43:2)

Blessed are they that mourn: for they shall be comforted (Matthew 5:4)

Take therefore no thought for the morrow: for the morrow shall take thought for the things of itself. Sufficient unto the day is the evil thereof. (Matthew 6:34)

Come unto me, all ye that labour and are heavy laden, and I will give you rest. Take my yoke upon you, and learn of me; for I am meek and lowly in heart: and ye shall find rest unto your souls. For my yoke is easy, and my burden is light. (Matthew 11:28–30)

Peace I leave with you, my peace I give unto you: not as the world giveth, give I unto you. Let not your heart be troubled, neither let it be afraid. (John 14:27)

And ye now therefore have sorrow: but I will see you again, and your heart shall rejoice, and your joy no man taketh from you. (John 16:22)

For I reckon that the sufferings of this present time are not worthy to be compared with the glory which shall be revealed in us. (Romans 8:18)

And we know that all things work together for good to them that love God, to them who are the called according to his purpose. For whom he did foreknow, he also did predestinate to be conformed to the image of his Son, that he might be the firstborn among many brethren. (Romans 8:28–29)

Blessed be God, even the Father of our Lord Jesus Christ, the Father of mercies, and the God of all comfort; Who comforteth us in all our tribulation, that we may be able to comfort them which are in any trouble, by the comfort wherewith we ourselves are comforted of God. (2 Corinthians 1:3–4)

Rejoice in the Lord alway: and again I say, Rejoice. Let your moderation be known unto all men. The Lord is at hand. Be careful for nothing; but in every thing by prayer and supplication with thanksgiving let your requests be made known unto God. And the peace of God, which passeth all understanding, shall keep your hearts and minds through Christ Jesus. Finally, brethren, whatsoever things are true, whatsoever things are honest, whatsoever things are just, whatsoever things are pure, whatsoever things are lovely, whatsoever things are of good report; if there be any virtue, and if there be any praise, think on these things. (Philippians 4:4–8)

For we have not an high priest which cannot be touched with the feeling of our infirmities; but was in all points tempted like as we are, yet without sin. Let us therefore come boldly unto the throne of grace, that we may obtain mercy, and find grace to help in time of need. (Hebrews 4:15-16)

Humble yourselves therefore under the mighty hand of God, that he may exalt you in due time: Casting all your care upon him; for he careth for you. (1 Peter 5:6–7)

And God shall wipe away all tears from their eyes; and there shall be no more death, neither sorrow, nor crying, neither shall there be any more pain: for the former things are passed away. (Revelation 21:4)

ENDNOTES

Session 1

1 Dr. Alan J. Noble develops this idea in his book-length essay "On Getting out of Bed: The Burden and Gift of Living" (Downers Grove, IL: InterVarsity Press, 2023).

2 Joni Eareckson Tada, *The Practice of the Presence of Jesus: Daily Meditations on the Nearness of Our Savior* (Colorado Springs, CO: Multnomah, 2023), xxix.

3 "How Wounds Heal," *Johns Hopkins Medicine*, accessed March 2, 2024, https://www.hopkinsmedicine.org/health/treatment-tests-and-therapies/how-wounds-heal; Noreen Iftikhar, "What to Expect During the 4 Stages of Wound Healing," *Healthline*, December 19, 2019, https://www.healthline.com/health/skin/stages-of-wound-healing#stages-of-wound-healing.

Session 2

1 Meg Bucher, "The Beauty of Seeking Both Joy and Happiness in Christ," *Bible Study Tools*, updated July 18, 2023, https://www.biblestudytools.com/bible-study/topical-studies/the-beauty-of-seeking-both-joy-and-happiness-in-christ.html.

2 C. S. Lewis, *A Grief Observed* (New York: HarperCollins, 2009 [1961]), Kindle edition.

3 Lewis, *A Grief Observed*, Kindle edition.

4 Lewis, *A Grief Observed*, Kindle edition

5 "A guide to getting through grief," *Harvard Health Publishing*, March 13, 2012, https://www.health.harvard.edu/blog_extra/a-guide-to-getting-through-grief.

Session 3

1 Greg Scheer, quoted in "Great is thy Faithfulness," *Hymnary.org*, accessed June 19, 2024 (1994), https://hymnary.org/text/great_is_thy_faithfulness_o_god_my_fathe.

2 Greg Scheer, *Hymnary.org*.

3 "Healing Your Brain After Loss: How Grief Rewires the Brain," *American Brain Foundation*, September 29, 2021, https://www.americanbrainfoundation.org/how-tragedy-affects-the-brain/.

Session 5

1 Albert Barnes, *Barnes' Notes on the New Testament*, ed. Ingram Cobbin (Grand Rapids, MI: Kregel Publications, 1962), 609.

Session 7

1 Bret Baier with Catherine Whitney, *To Rescue the Constitution: George Washington and the Fragile American Experiment* (New York, NY and Boston, MA: Mariner Books, 2023), 15-29.

Session 8

1 Joni Eareckson Tada, *A Place of Healing: Wrestling with the Mysteries of Suffering, Pain, and God's Sovereignty* (Colorado Springs, CO: David C. Cook, 2010), 34.

2 Tada, *A Place of Healing,* 52

3 Makoto Fujimura, *Art and Faith: A Theology of Making* (New Haven, CT: Yale University Press, 2021), Kindle edition; D. Christopher Ralston, "Shining through the Cracks," *Sapientia,* April 21, 2022, https://henrycenter.tiu.edu/2022/04/shining-through-the-cracks/.

4 Tada, *A Place of Healing,* 70-71.

5 "Gracia Burnham Testimony," YouTube video, 20:20, posted by Cross Con, February 3, 2022, https://youtu.be/eZXT6SeMVUY.

Session 9

1 James Clear, *Atomic Habits: An Easy & Proven Way to Build Good Habits & Break Bad Ones* (New York: Penguin, 2018), 6.

2 Clear, *Atomic Habits,*142-143

3 *Clear, Atomic Habits,* 15.

Session 10

1 Historical and biographical details for this devotional drawn from the following sources: *Corrie ten Boom, The Hiding Place* (Grand Rapids, MI: Chosen Books, 2011); "Corrie ten Boom," *Wikipedia.com,* accessed May 5, 2024, https://en.wikipedia.org/wiki/Corrie_ten_Boom.

2 Corrie ten Boom, *The Hiding Place,* 210.

Session 11

1 "Speaking of Psychology: Why we need hope, with Chan Hellman, PhD, and Jacqueline Mattis, PhD," [Podcast], *Speaking of Psychology Podcast,* episode 265, December 2023, American Psychological Association, https://www.apa.org/news/podcasts/speaking-of-psychology/hope.

2 Carol Graham, "The New Science of Hope: Economists are beginning to understand how aspiration shapes life outcomes," *The Atlantic,* April 25, 2023, https://www.theatlantic.com/ideas/archive/2023/04/economics-hope-optimism-despair/673835/.

3 Dan J. Tomasulo, "The New Science of Hope: Hope is the only positive emotion that requires negativity or uncertainty," *Psychology Today.com,* July 31, 2022, https://www.psychologytoday.com/us/blog/the-healing-crowd/202207/the-new-science-hope.

4 "The Left-Handed Whopper," *Hoaxes.com,* accessed May 28, 2024, https://hoaxes.org/af_database/permalink/the_left-handed_whopper/.

5 Dan Fletcher, "The Left-Handed Whopper—1998," *Time.com,* April 1, 2011, https://content.time.com/time/specials/packages/article/0,28804,1888721_1888719_1888662,00.html.

6 "Charles and Susannah Spurgeon's Tomb at West Norwood Cemetery," YouTube video, 5:21, posted by Paul Chappell, May 21, 2024, https://youtu.be/p7YPYxdM2BA.

7 "Charles Spurgeon," *Wikipedia.com,* accessed May 29, 2024, https://en.wikipedia.org/wiki/Charles_Spurgeon.

8 Kate Springer, "Man who visited every country without flying has finally returned home," *CNN.com,* August 2, 2023, https://www.cnn.com/travel/thor-pedersen-visited-every-country-returns-home-intl-hnk/index.html.

9 C. S. Lewis, *The Weight of Glory: And Other Addresses, Collected Letters of C. S. Lewis* (New York: HarperCollins, 2009), 29.

Session 12

1 Details for this historic fire were drawn from the following sources: Dakin Andone, "The largest wildfire in California's modern history is finally out, more than 6 months after it started," *CNN.com,* June 2, 2018, https://www.cnn.com/2018/06/02/us/thomas-fire-officially-out/index.html; Faith Karimi and Steve Almasy, "California mudslides: Death toll rises after searchers find body," *CNN.com,* January 13, 2018, https://www.cnn.com/2018/01/12/us/southern-california-mudslides/index.html; "Heavy Rain Pummeled California, Triggering Debris Flows From Recent Wildfire Burn Areas (RECAP)," *Weather.com,* January 10, 2018, https://weather.com/forecast/regional/news/2018-01-09-california-flooding-debris-flows-burn-areas; California Governor's Office of Emergency Services, "Montecito Mudslides Anniversary, Reflections Through Images," *Cal OES News,* accessed June 05, 2024, https://news.caloes.ca.gov/montecito-mudslides-anniversary-reflections-through-images/.

PAUL CHAPPELL is the senior pastor of the Lancaster Baptist Church and president of West Coast Baptist College in Lancaster, California. His biblical vision has led the church to become one of the most dynamic independent Baptist churches in the nation, and his Christ-centered leadership philosophy has become a model for hundreds of future leaders. He has been married to his wife, Terrie, since 1980 and is the father of four married children who are all serving in Christian ministry.

ADDITIONAL RESOURCES FOR ENCOURAGEMENT

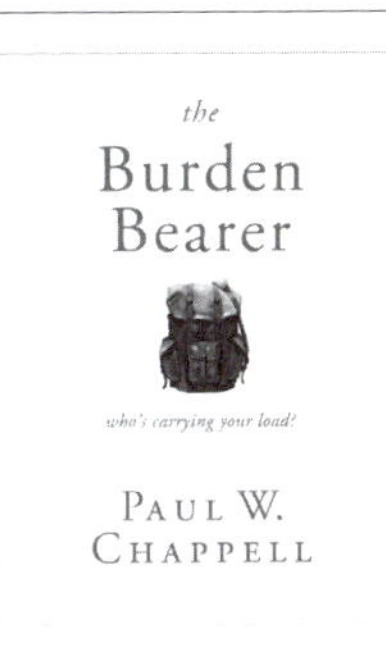

The Burden Bearer by Paul Chappell

One Lifetime, Limited Resources, Eternal Priorities

The allegory in these pages will captivate your heart, delight your soul, and profoundly change your life. Follow the main character—Carrier—on his journey with the Burden Bearer, and discover the Christian life and relationship with Jesus that you were meant to enjoy!

The Resilient Life by Paul Chappell

Overcoming the Crises and Anxieties of Life through Christ

With over four decades of pastoral ministry experience, Dr. Paul Chappell writes with understanding and compassion for the tribulations of life, coupled with insight into the promises of God and help from His Word to enable us to overcome.

How to Get Through What You'll Never Get Over by Bill Prater

Walking through Grief by the Grace of God

Have you ever experienced a grief so deep that you knew it would forever change you? In these pages, Pastor Bill Prater shares from his own experience of losing his adult son in an accident and how God's grace is sufficient—enough—to lead you through grief and loss.

FOR MORE GROUP STUDIES, VISIT

STRIVINGTOGETHER.COM